ENLIGHTENED VIEW OF NATIVE AMERICANS ON FILM

Katina M. Stamper

Enlightened View of Native Americans on Film

Copyright © 2011 by Katina M. Stamper

All rights reserved. No part of this book may be reproduced or transmitted in any form or by any means without written permission of the author.

ISBN 978-0-9836529-0-8

Acknowledgments

I would like to express my sincere appreciation to Dr. Ronald Janke for opening my eyes to the true and parallel history of Native Americans.

I would also like to thank my loving, supportive, and patient husband Pete for encouraging me to pursue my passion.

Contents

Preface 1

1. Assimilation 3
2. The Searchers 9
3. Ulzana's Raid 15
4. Indians as Mascots 21
5. The Return of Navajo Boy 25
6. Geronimo 31
7. Geronimo and the Apache Resistance 37
8. They Died With Their Boots On 43
9. Little Big Man 55
10. Dances With Wolves 65
11. War Party 71
12. The Education of Little Tree 77
13. Thunderheart 85
14. Soldier Blue 97

Conclusion 103
Bibliography 107

Preface

Although I am not a scholarly expert on Native American Indians, I have had my eyes opened to widespread inaccuracies that plague our historical texts and skew our perceptions of reality in the media. As an adult college student, my historical view of our nation was shattered when I took a course concerning Indians and the Media to satisfy my Diversity requirement. Although I was always fascinated by Native American Art and Culture, I couldn't have imagined that most of what I understood to be true was based on inaccurate portrayals in various forms of media. It has also occurred to me that when I hear about protection of rights and individual liberties, Native American Indians are almost never mentioned. My goal in publishing these essays is to encourage you to question what you have been taught, challenge what you see and hear in the media, and be sensitive to the hardships that centuries of Indians have endured. Even if you don't view all of the films/documentaries that I have chosen to present, I will provide an overview of the plots and pertinent dialogue. I invite you to view the history of the Native American Indians with a fresh set of eyes and question what you think you know about their history and culture.

Group of Omaa boys in cadet uniforms, Carlisle Indian School, Pennsylvania.

Photographed by J. N. Choate, ca. 1880.

Courtesy National Archives, photo no. 153 (American Indian Select List)

Chapter 1
Assimilation

Carlisle Indian Industrial School practice (1879-1918) was to, "...give each student a uniform, cut his hair, teach him English above all, you know, forbid him from speaking his native language, remove him as far as possible from the center of his real existence, his spiritual existence, put him in a strange place, you know a place where he has no advantage whatsoever, and he will become what you want him to become. You can draw a picture and let him look at it and slowly he will transform himself into the image that he sees there...." (Landis) This experiment in social transformation was perhaps the dawning of a misguided social conscience that replaced genocidal occurrences at the hands of the military. After two centuries of extermination of massive populations of Indians, either through war or indirectly through white man's diseases, outright physical genocide was replaced by social genocide.

Perhaps it was highly ironic that the Carlisle, Pennsylvania Industrial School for Indians was an abandoned army post. It wasn't enough that so many tribes of Indians had been virtually decimated through years of displacement, disease, and savage murders at the hands of the whites. If the Indians couldn't be driven any further out of the white man's world, then the Indians must be suppressed from the inside out.

Through this social experiment, before and after pictures would be taken to show the transformation from savage Indian to a civilized state of being. The misguided participants hell-bent on Christianizing the wild Indians equated development of intelligence with evolution of appearance as though the young children who had been ripped from their homes and families weren't capable of learning in their own environments. It was believed that separation from their families was the key to transforming these children into good little Indians with Christian morals and values. Most would describe this environment as a lonely prison.

"School life was modeled after military life. Uniforms were issued for the boys, the girls dressed in Victorian-style dresses. Shoes were required, as no moccasins were allowed. The boys and girls were organized into companies with officers who took charge of drill. The children marched to and from their classes, and to the dining hall for meals. No one was allowed to speak their native tongue. Discipline was strictly enforced – military style. There was regular drill practice and the children were ranked, with the officers in command. A court system was organized in the hierarchical style of a military justice system, with students determining the consequences for offenses. The most severe punishment was to be confined to the guardhouse." (Landis) Punishment would have been employed frequently for mild occurrences and these poor children would have to endure long stints in solitary confinement. Former military officer from the 10th Cavalry who

ASSIMILATION

served in the Indian Territory, Richard Henry Pratt, believed and professed that, "You must kill the Indian to save the man." (Landis)

After Quaker and other religious groups began programs to indoctrinate Indians into the ways of white man's civilization, Pratt decided that he wanted to start an influential school of his own. In an address to a convention of Baptist ministers in 1883 Pratt wrote: "In Indian civilization I am a Baptist, because I believe in immersing the Indians in our civilization and when we get them under holding them there until they are thoroughly soaked." (Landis) Thus he lobbied the government and gained wealthy supporters in his newly found battle against the Indians.

It wasn't enough that he took these children from their homelands far away from their families on the Plains. He would also further strip them of their ancestral heritage by forbidding their old manner of dress and replace it with military uniforms and clunky boots to replace their moccasins. Another central part of the initiation process was to cut the Indian children's long hair with utter disregard for what this meant to do so. "For the Lakhota (Sioux), the cutting of hair was symbolic of mourning and there was much wailing and lamenting which lasted into the night." (Landis) Although it isn't documented, I wonder how many children received punishments or time in solitary confinement for white man's ignorance with respect to Indian beliefs and customs such as this, for which the children would surely be lonely, scared, and bewildered.

It must have been devastating for these children to be ripped from their families to be sent to such a harsh environment where they had to abandon all they had ever known. Upon arrival, no provisions had yet been arranged for their care and they had to sleep on the cold floor like dogs for days until other arrangements could be made. I wonder if provisions were simply late or if this was part of the overall plan to shock the children into utter submission. Perhaps the most disheartening of all might have been the forced abandonment of their Indian names. Since Indians were very connected to the Earth and names were bestowed with a high level of meaning, this would be the final act to separate the children from their homelands and put a wedge between them and the natural environment. As a replacement, children were asked to choose from a series of names on a blackboard but most couldn't read and didn't know what any of them meant. In reality, for those who might have been able to read, the Christian names would probably not hold meaning for them anyway.

Overall, this social experiment was not only an attempt to civilize wild Indians but also to immerse students in an industrial way of life. In a highly progressive industrial society, individual accomplishments and successes are highly esteemed above group cohesion. This would be a very foreign concept to children who had just come from such cohesive tribes, composed not only of strong family ties but also extended families. The Indians worked together to create a stable and nurturing society: They didn't suppress others for personal gain. To stress the importance of work, students would attend school for half of the day and work the other half in various trades. I wonder just how many whites profited from this child exploitation in the days before unionization and child labor laws.

Twenty-Five such schools sprang up in 13 states controlled by whistles and bugles. Living by white man's patterns would have also been very foreign and a difficult adjustment for these children who lived based on the cycles of the Earth, not the rigid time schedules of an industrialized society. Some students would come to believe they were in fact soldiers. "Enrollment at the Indian School began to swell as more and more nations' children were recruited. The original group of 82 grew to yearly averages of 1,000 students, necessitating more living and classroom space...a cemetery was also needed." (Landis) As many students contracted diseases such as smallpox and tuberculosis, others became ill under the highly stressful separation and rigid living conditions. Many students died and some were not sent back to their families or homelands for burial; however, they were buried in the cemetery erected on the school's property, doomed to be connected to the school forever.

This social experiment in Indian transformation was truly an act of social genocide. White man's notions of progress in an industrialized society further suppressed the Indian way of life in an indirect attempt to kill the remaining Indian populations, one child at a time. For students who had completed successful transformations into good little white children, visits with family would have been awkward as a wedge would permanently be driven between the old Indian ways and the newly indoctrinated ways of the white man. The great Indian Sitting Bull once said, "If the Great Spirit had desired me to be a white man he would have made me so in the first place." (Welker)

Sitting Bull (Tatonka-I-Yatanka), a Hunkpapa Sioux.

Photographed by David F. Barry, ca. 1885.

**Courtesy National Archives, photo no. 124
(American Indian Select List)**

Chapter 2
The Searchers

Although the John Ford movie, *The Searchers (1956)* is visually captivating and provides a window into the old west, it is plagued by inaccurate stereotyping of North American Indians. The Indians are portrayed as villains and John Wayne who plays Ethan Edwards, his nephew Martin Pawley, and his supporting cast of settlers and Texas Rangers, are portrayed as victorious heroes who must fight these villains for their survival against attacks. The prejudicial tone of the movie against the Indians is set early and is further dramatized by gross inaccuracies that have done much to further false stereotypes of Native Americans.

The first very strong example of racial stereotyping is the portrayal of Indians as predatory savages who attack the settlers in an unwarranted fashion. This is perpetuated by the successful trick that they perform by leading Edwards and his fellow band of investigators out to find the missing and slaughtered cattle belonging to one of the settlers. This trick is a mere ploy to draw the protective forces out to leave the women and children helpless at their homesteads. The Indians are then portrayed as murdering beasts who not only viciously kill Edwards' brother, sister-in-law, and blood-nephew but also kidnap his two nieces Lucy and Debra.

This leads to the second assumption that Indians kidnap white women to fulfill their sexual desires. Later in the film, Edwards tries to hide the discovery of his niece Lucy's body, for which he must eventually admit because her fiancé Brad believes that he sees her and plans a rescue. Edwards also implies that she has been raped prior to her murder. Although never bluntly stated, the intense dramatic acting does nothing to dispel this fact in any viewer's mind. It is also implied that Debra is still alive because of her tender age and that she will remain a slave to be raised as the Indian's own until she is old enough to be married or engage in sexual intercourse. Again, this is not clearly stated, perhaps because of the decade in which this picture was filmed. However, there is a sullen outlook for what the future holds for Debra if they do not rescue her. Not only do her rescuers believe that to be indoctrinated as an Indian is a horrible thing for which an individual is almost deemed inhuman but also that a woman can utterly lose her mind after being subjected to rape and brutal Indian practices. As Edwards states in the movie, "The women ain't white any more, now they're Comanche...Even the most civilized person can turn insane under these circumstances." The women that the military troops have rescued and that Edwards and Pawley are scrutinizing to try and find Debra are all portrayed as highly insane for which they will never be normal or white again.

Additionally, negative views of Indian women are expressed in this film. In an extremely foolish skit in which Pawley is trading with the Indians, he unknowingly trades for a wife. "Look," as she is called, is portrayed as a quiet, submissive, and subservient woman who neither possesses a mind of her own nor any common sense. Indian women are too often depicted in films as powerless sex objects who are slaves to men. This is refuted by many who claim that historically, Indian societies have been much more communal and in many cases matriarchal. Women have even had the authority in certain cases to give rulings against those voted on by male tribal councils. Whether portrayed as the subservient idiot, fat old lady, or young submissive sex object, only in the rarest of cases are Indian women portrayed in a positive light.

Another portrayal that I find utterly disturbing is that of the mentally challenged Mose Harper. He is a caring and loyal individual who does assist Edwards and the Texas Rangers at different points in the movie. However, he is also mistreated at times and he is even kicked in the backside by Edwards. When he receives ill words or treatment, he responds by saying, "Thank you kindly." My heart aches for this character: All he wants is a roof over his head and a rocking chair by the fire. In the end, to my satisfaction, the Jorgensen family takes him in and provides for his care. However, I am saddened at all of the years of longing and ridicule that he has to endure to finally find someone who will take him in.

Also disturbing are the physical misrepresentations through various battles between Edwards' posse and the Indians. Accompanied by his ill-related nephew Martin Pawley, played by Jeffrey Hunter, and the Texas Rangers, the Indians are portrayed as relentless opponents who: don feathers on their heads; smear their faces with war paint; speak unintelligently; plunder; kill at will; and, keep collections of scalps as symbols of honor and pride. These additional stereotypes are believed to be true by the characters in the movie, especially Edwards, who seems to know much about the Comanche Indians they pursue. It is this racist view that facilitates much drama and conflict between Edwards and his nephew Martin Pawley, who is a quarter Indian. Edwards rejects him upon their first meeting prior to the attack on his family and only after years of searching together for Debra, seems to warm up to his nephew slightly. Unfortunately in its time, and perhaps even now, Ethan Edwards' character is seen as an idyllic figure of strength and masculinity without addressing the prejudicial Achilles Heel that he possesses.

In addition to the above-mentioned physical depictions of the Indians, distorted views about character and of Indian beliefs are prevalent in the movie. One example occurs early in the film when Edwards, Pawley, and the Texas Rangers set out in search of the missing cattle. Pawley expresses that something seems to be strange about the trail that they are on, to which Edwards replies that it is just his suspicious nature as an "Injun" which is a highly offensive reference to Native Americans. Another example is when the men stumble upon the fresh grave of an Indian underneath a boulder. As Lucy's betrothed angrily pelts the deceased with a large rock, Edwards pulls out a gun and shoots the Indian's eyes. The falsely created myth is that if the Indian's eyes are gone, he will be forced to aimlessly wander the spirit world forever. Is this a false creation by ignorant movie executives or a myth that has been passed down by white men through years of oral tradition? Regardless of whether or not it is rooted in history, the very fact that it is believed and portrayed in the film connects with the human psyche and is unjustly adapted as truth.

Just as the stereotypical views of Indians as suspicious and superstitious are portrayed in the movie, so too is a widely held view of tribal chiefs. During the attack on Edwards' family early in the movie, Scar, the Comanche Chief, first appears standing over Debra at her grandmother's grave. He is an evil, lurking presence over the innocent little girl as he gives the signal for the others to attack. Scar is also involved in other conflicts, for which he places a full feather headdress on top of his head prior to battle and wears war paint on his face. Later when Edwards and Pawley track him down after years of pursuits at his camp, he shocks them by not only showing them many scalps that he has collected, one of which belongs to Pawley's own mother, but also that he has Debra display them. In this climactic movie moment, Scar perpetuates the belief that all Indians are scalp hunters and he is almost boastful that he can parade his captive Debra, knowing that they have been searching for her all of these years. These factors combined, do much to imprint the image of an Indian savage chieftain that is malicious, yet cartoon-like in his manner of appearance.

Unfortunately, years of false depictions in movies have created a laundry list of gross inaccuracies that have been adapted as truth through erroneous physical, cultural, and religious portrayals. Although the filmmakers might not have intended to facilitate such widespread injustices, they have done much damage to the historical representation and preservation of an already misunderstood population of people, perhaps beyond repair. The consequences of these otherwise "entertaining" movies have taken years to be fully realized, perhaps much too late to alter people's perceptions; however, efforts at correction must still be continually sought.

Chapter 3
Ulzana's Raid

Although John Ford's movie *The Searchers* is plagued by grossly inaccurate stereotypes of Native American Indians, *Ulzana's Raid* (1972) is a blatantly irresponsible misrepresentation of Apache Indians by filmmakers to sensationalize incidence of raids against settlers. Whereas, *The Searchers* is more subtle in its prejudicial tone and develops its themes throughout the movie, *Ulzana's Raid* drops a racist atomic bomb almost immediately following the opening credits. Ulzana and his so-called war party are utterly dehumanized and portrayed as animal-like savages with no conscience and who are incapable of feeling remorse for their predatory actions.

From the earliest discussions between the military officers in this film, these Apache Indians are accused of incidence of rape, torture, and murder. This leaves no room for doubt in the viewer's mind that this war party acts on relentless pursuits of evil with utter disregard for human life. Even though one of the officers is hesitant to send troops, the central character of the seasoned scout, McIntosh, played by Burt Lancaster, stresses the urgent nature based on the atrocities committed by Ulzana and his warriors. Indoctrination of hate is already set in motion early in this poor excuse of an "entertaining" film.

In the quest for information about Ulzana, McIntosh and an interpreter question two old Indian men. However, they are portrayed as liars and thieves as they steal the cigars used for bribery when left alone. McIntosh even goes so far as to say, "...half of what they speak is lies and the other half ain't true." Dishonesty and thievery are further added to the ever-growing list of negative characteristics of this Indian population as it is asserted that 100 % of what they speak is lies. They are even repeatedly referred to as hostiles. The self conscious becomes a metaphoric victim of repetitive attempts at programming to hate these people even before they hit the screen.

If there is any doubt left in one's mind that the Apaches will be too harshly presented, grossly irresponsible acts of visual dramatization squelch the hope that there will be a plot twist in which the Indians may actually be redeemed. The Indians attack fleeing settlers, without cause, as they attempt to reach safety at the fort. However, some don't make it. As a mother and son ride along in their carriage, they are attacked by Ulzana and his war party. After first shooting the horse, they viciously kill the mother, sitting right next to her frightened son. Next, they put a bullet in the brain of the officer who attempts to protect these fleeing settlers. Rather than cut away and leave anything to the imagination, as they would have in *The Searchers*, they show in very graphic detail, the bullet as it strikes the officer in the head. As if this isn't bad enough, the animalistic savages that the filmmakers want the viewer to see, pull the heart right out of the officer's chest with their bare hands and then dance around and toss it with glee. This disgusting display is followed by scenes of the Indians stealing not only from the wagon but also from the dead woman's body. They even force the little boy to remove his mother's ring and give it to them. They do let him live, however, but as McIntosh later states, "...they must have left him on a whim, the Apache generally act on a whim...." The young Christian Lieutenant then points out that at least the woman wasn't raped, to which McIntosh replies, "...only because she was dead before they got to her...."

The haunting image of the little boy sitting over his murdered mother is a gut-wrenching scene; however, the scope of the raid is not fully realized until his father is attacked back at the homestead. The first mode of attack occurs when the dog is shot with bows and arrows and the camera captures the scene as the dog continues to heavily breathe and fight for his life. When the father realizes what has happened, he attempts to lock himself in the house and grabs his gun for protection. The Indians then set fire to the house in an attempt either to draw him out or to clear a path in. However, in an act of trickery, the war party acts as though they have fled the scene while the sound of what appears to be trumpets gives the settler the impression that the cavalry has come to save him. To his demise, he leaves the safety of his home and the next glimpse of this poor victim is utterly repulsive, as he is shown tied and burned alive. Perhaps more disturbing is the image of the dog's tail which has been severed and stuck in his mouth. In response to this discovery, McIntosh says, "...the Apache have a sense of humor and just find things funny...."

ENLIGHTENED VIEW OF NATIVE AMERICANS ON FILM

In a very short period of time, the filmmakers dehumanize these Apache Indians to the point that they are viewed as utterly animalistic and pure evil. Whether engaging in relentless pursuits of murder and theft, or taking pleasure in dismembering human beings and animals, the actions of these fictional characters leaves no room for doubt that they are pure evil. I neither find this film entertaining nor am I able to watch it without feeling full of anger and despair. The makers of this picture acted irresponsibly in an attempt to push the envelope and increase revenues at the expense of an already displaced and abused Indian population. Racism is the overriding theme of this movie, PERIOD!

http://indianmascots.com/

Chapter 4
Indians as Mascots

Mascots used for schools, businesses, and other forms in the media are not necessarily morally wrong and can induce a positive feeling toward a particular institution. However, the fact that Native American Indians are still so widely utilized and marginalized in this process is quite disturbing. Protected members of society, such as African Americans, Hispanics, Asians, and other ethnic minorities, along with religious groups, are no longer portrayed for sport or amusement; yet, too many individuals don't understand the harm in continuing to portray Indians in a cartoonish sense.

I find it quite alarming that my home state of Indiana is one of the worst offenders in the United States for utilization of Indian mascots. However, I can confirm that through my years of schooling in Portage, Indiana, I was a Fegely Middle School Warrior and a Portage High School Indian. The students at the other middle school in Portage were, and may still be, referred to as the Willowcreek Braves. I am ashamed to admit the widespread nature of the images that appeared on t-shirts and other items sold to promote school spirit and to fund extra-curricular programs. As a cheerleader, we even had a few cheers that incorporated Indian themes. Although I don't know of anyone who intentionally degraded Native American Indians, I now realize the implications of the offensive nature of our actions.

Charlene Teters, a Native American Indian: advocate; artist; educator; and lecturer began her mission to promote understanding of and action against the offensive and harmful nature in using Indian mascots as a graduate student at the University of Illinois at Urbana-Champaign in 1988. Although University of Illinois officials and trustees have argued that the mascot is inspirational and uplifting, Teters argues that the use of sacred rituals and manner of dress reserved for the highest tribal chieftains is a mockery and has damaging consequences. Her family has even felt the pain and shame of seeing sacred and historical customs depicted at sporting events for entertainment purposes. She says that during the first game she took her children to in 1989, "...my kids sank in their seats...my daughter tried to become invisible...my son tried to laugh...." (Teters) The mascot's costume was very authentic, wearing a buckskin outfit and eagle feather headdress. However, this sacred vestment and ritualistic dance is supposed to be reserved for tribal chiefs, not used as a means of entertainment. This mockery marginalizes the sacred religious customs of Native American Indians.

Her initial feelings of sadness turned to anger as she witnessed the pain and embarrassment that her children felt. They were brought up to respect ancient customs and practices. Rather than sit and do nothing, she felt compelled to act and began to shout, "American Indians are human beings not mascots!" (Teters) She was then heckled and told to shut up and to get out. Other individuals that have been interviewed say that she should not be offended and that no harm is being done. I recall an interview, in which one man refuted Teters' objections to mascots and considered Indians to be foreigners because he was an Illinois resident and a tax payer and believed there was no cause to be upset but if there was he didn't care. Does this man understand what the "native" in Native American Indian stands for?

It is for these reasons that Teters has made it her mission to change racist practices and alter prejudicial attitudes. She has been an advocate for change and diversity not only at the University of Illinois but also to promote widespread awareness. She wants to inform the public that these images of mockery can be harmful to the self-esteem and identity of American Indians. In addition, the portrayals are all too often accepted as truthful, regardless of inaccuracies that occur. The Indians are already misunderstood by the mainstream and wrongful depictions can do much to further this misunderstanding and scrutiny. For an already displaced population of people, fighting to save historical religious custom and practices, this can do much psychological and emotional harm. Creation and perpetuation of false stereotypes is dangerous to the preservation and continuation of Native American Indian history and culture.

Although most do not intend to engage in racial practices by participating in events that utilize Indian mascots, awareness of the implications of these actions is of the utmost importance. Why aren't Native American Indians a protected group as African Americans and other ethnic groups are? Why don't people understand that mocking an Indian is just has harmful as mocking any other ethnic group? Does anyone realize that the Native American Indians were here long before any European settlers? The answer is that people do know but the answers are locked in a defensive self-conscience and not at the forefront of thought. It is the responsibility of all individuals to overlook stereotypical portrayals of Indians and to fully realize the harm in allowing these injustices to continue against an underrepresented and negligently unprotected native population.

Chapter 5
The Return of Navajo Boy

It is no secret that the vast population of diverse tribes of Indians have been exploited and continually exposed to discriminatory practices ever since white men first settled the new world. Injustices are not simply rooted in history; however, they are an ever-present consequence of the unfair treatment of this unprotected group of people. The documentary *The Return of Navajo Boy* (2000) blaringly depicts several hardships forced upon the Cly family and their fellow Navajo Indians in Monument Valley, Utah.

While watching the John Ford movie *The Searchers,* I was utterly unaware that the Cly family and their fellow Navajo Indians were not only extras in this film but also that they were so regularly photographed and filmed by outsiders. It angered me to find out that even to this day, the images taken so long ago are still generating profits via postcards, movies, and other forms of merchandise and media for which none of those photographed or filmed have ever seen a penny. As the family matriarch Elsie Mae Cly Begay has stated, "There are thousands of pictures of us, but we never got to say anything." They have no control over how the thousands of images are being used, have never shared in any profits, and have not been able to fully narrate life as it existed for them when the images were captured.

The most photographed of all individuals during this period of the 1940s and 1950s was Grandma Cly, simply called "Navajo Woman." I wonder if anyone will ever understand the significance of this elder woman's position within the Navajo community outside of the images of her daily grinding of cornmeal. I wonder if anyone realizes that many Indian communities have been historically matriarchal in nature. I wonder if anyone has stopped and realized that this woman was actually once a living breathing individual beloved by her family and community. I wonder if anyone realizes that more than likely, there is no formal consensual contract authorizing the use of these images. I wonder if at all possible, this family can sue for reimbursement for years of illegal usage of their images. Finally, I wonder how this massive exploitation has gone on for so long and how we can allow it to continue today.

Another point of contention that absolutely makes my blood boil is the exploitation of Navajo Indians in uranium mining, even involving young boys. These human beings were never informed of the risks involved in this kind of work and now, have paid the ultimate price with their lives as many have died from lung cancer. The astonishing thing is that even those individuals who have not worked in the mines have also succumbed to the disease. Generations past, as well as the current population surrounding these mines have been at risk for so long that many have become ill and died.

The government is aware of this widespread problem and has claimed that they will pay for mine workers who have contracted cancer; however, most of those affected have never seen a penny. Bernie Cly had his lung cut in half from this cancer and was never reimbursed because the government said he became ill from smoking tobacco, not from uranium exposure. According to his account, "He never smoked white man's tobacco...that which he has is for rituals and is a natural smoke." In addition, water and environmental samples have been taken for which these people have never been given the results of the findings. The mining companies were supposed to come back and clean up the areas involved but at the time of this documentary, still had not lived up to their promise. Rather, the Indians themselves have been instructed that they are responsible for testing for radiation and they will probably have to leave. Once again these Native Americans are faced with two difficult options, stay and risk exposure to deadly uranium poisoning or leave their historical home for which they believe has a living soul that they themselves are a part of.

When the government completed testing of their drinking water, they never came back with results. Were they afraid to come back to the area and risk exposure to themselves or were they afraid that the findings would be too explosive and too costly to allow to be made public? In either case, approximately 200 people who live in the area, some as far as 30 miles away, must drive to a communal well for their daily drinking water. As if the injustice of having to drive such a great distance for an essential part of daily life isn't enough, there is absolutely no surety that the water is even safe to drink. These unfortunate souls are forced to play a game of Russian roulette with each breath that they take and with each drink of water essential for life itself.

The government places no value on the lives of these people and has done much through its actions and inactions not only to endanger but also to displace members of the Navajo, in particular the Cly family. When the young John Wayne Cly, Elsie's brother, was two years old, he was taken away because his mother was ill. It was promised that he would be returned, per the mother's request once she was better but that promise was never upheld. Rather, after her death, and for so many decades, Elsie and her family longed to find John. There was always a void in their family and an aching in their hearts. It was only through the reemergence of the old film footage that John was reunited with his family.

As John recalls his childhood, he never felt any attachment and never quite fit in. He was also, it appears, the victim of abuse by his foster family. As an injustice to his heritage, he was never exposed to this history or customs of his people. He was also never allowed to speak his native language or even acknowledge his ethnicity. When he came of age upon graduating high school, his family, if you can call them that, sent him on his way and told him he was old enough to leave. However, he was never prepared as to how to deal with the world and through his difficulties, turned to alcohol. Ironically, even though he was not in direct contact with his own people, he shared the same fate as so many Navajo men and boys who ended up in the uranium mines. He always wanted to find his family but never knew if they would accept him back after living with the white man ways. He even went into a local general store to look through many post cards to see if he recognized anyone that someone might still know how to contact. Ironically, it was one of the films from so many decades back that helped John Wayne Cly, named for the major motion picture star, find his way back to his family. In the heart-warming, tear-jerking reunion, the little Navajo Boy, now a man is reunited with his family. He can now feel whole, where he had once been plagued by emptiness.

Gross injustices have plagued Indian populations from their first encounters with people from other lands. They have been displaced, exploited, and discriminated against as though they are alien to this land. Regardless of their status as truly native to the Americas, they continually suffer at the hands of the media, governmental agencies, and by corporations and private businesses that profit from their pain. The consequences of these gross atrocities are inaccurate stereotyping, loss of self-esteem and identity, and on a much larger scale lack of preservation of historical customs and practices. The psychological effects of which may never be fully understood to the detriment of the much larger human society.

Apache rancheria with two men holding rifles.

Photographed by Camillus S. Fly

Courtesy National Archives, photo no. 75 (American Indian Select List)

Chapter 6
Geronimo

The Paramount picture, *Geronimo (1940)*, misrepresents this historic Medicine Man and his people as evil savages who live as inhuman and reprehensible beings. This film also depicts Geronimo as a villainous creature with murderous intentions and utter revenge in his heart. However, the white characters are shown in loving relationships, displayed with great depth, experience traumatic loss and sorrow, and are victims of the Indians.

Just as the movie *Ulzana's Raid* leaves no room for doubt that the Indians are evil and inhuman savages, so too does this film not leave any room for doubt in the viewer's mind that the whites are the good guys and the Indians are the bad guys. During a brief set of interviews preceding the movie, the director Paul H. Sloane, clearly states that "You need conflict and Indians generally fit in the bad side." In addition, historically in motion pictures, Indian characters were not even played by real Indians. It was believed, according to the 1915 publication The Dangers of Employing Redskins as Movie Actors by Ernest Alfred Dench, that they had the capacity to act too violently toward the white characters in fight sequences and that additional guards were necessary if they were on set. These ridiculous notions furthered promotion of white actors to play Indian parts while it was foolishly believed that Indians could not adequately adapt to Indian parts.

However in *Geronimo,* a real Indian, Victor Daniels, a.k.a. Chief Thundercloud, plays the title character. Although this is a monumental event in the casting of an Indian in a lead role, he received bottom billing in the movie. Racial billing seems more the norm for this movie than is the usual practice of billing based on order of appearance or level of the role within the picture. In addition, his character rarely speaks or shows any expression or emotion. He is portrayed as a stone-cold character with a callous face and fear-provoking presence. According to Dench, "To act as an Indian is the easiest thing possible, for the Redskin is practically motionless." (Cruel.com) This belief gives no depth or soul to Geronimo in this film.

Geronimo is portrayed as a murderous villain with utter revenge in his heart. Perhaps the only somewhat truthful fact, that receives a brief second of screen time, is that Geronimo's family is killed. The act is not shown, no emotion or sense of loss is portrayed, and no bonds of family are expressed. The untruthful accompanying facts are that he is said to have slaughtered many people and will not stop until he kills at least 1,000 white men. In addition, the Indians are shown as inhuman savages that constantly murder and scalp their victims. The bombardment of newspaper reports of these reprehensible acts in the film only further the unjust myths and acts as propaganda to sway the viewer's psyche. In truth, the Indians would not have been so well armed with repeating shotguns and as great in numbers: It would have been the army who would have outmanned and outgunned the Indians.

Also, it is so frequently overlooked that the white characters are shown as individuals full of emotion and bound by meaningful relationships. The young lieutenant, Jack Steele, enters the fort where his father, General Steele is in command, in a quest to be reunited and get to know his long-lost father. Longing is a human emotion for which this young man wants to get to know himself, perhaps by getting to know his father. He is also full of enthusiasm and anxious to get a meaningful assignment to prove his worthiness as a soldier. His facial expressions and range of emotions are well pronounced and pivotal in the development of this character. He begins as a light-hearted and tender young man and develops into a seasoned military officer who is a little more hardened by his losses and experiences.

When first introduced to Lt. Steele's mother and fiancé, one can immediately see the bond that he has with his mother and that she has a difficult time letting him go. She holds him tightly and gazes into his eyes full of fear that she will never see him again. It is a moving moment between mother and son that emphasizes the bonds of motherly love. In a tender on-screen moment, he also says goodbye to his fiancé and begs her promise to take care of his mother. Although it is yet another difficult goodbye, it pales in comparison to the emotion shared between mother and son. Perhaps this is to emphasize the tender age and innocence of Lt. Steele and is the starting point of his on-screen development.

As days and weeks go by, General Steele refuses to see his son and to give him any assignments. Lt. Steele's tender light begins to dim as he becomes disheartened by his father's disinterest in getting to know him and disallowing the opportunity to prove himself worthy as a soldier. In an impetuous act, he prepares his resignation and sends for his mother and fiancé, which proves to be a horrible mistake. In an ironic twist of fate, Lt. Steele is going to defy his father's orders and leave the fort to meet his family and resign his position to head to California with the group of rescued settlers. However, he is too late to save his family, for the Indians attack the wagon, shooting and killing, at close range, his mother, and severely injuring his fiancé. This great loss hardens Lt. Steele and revenge becomes his quest. The earlier portrayal of bonds of motherly love highlights the sense of great loss for this white man.

As the other military officials approach the scene of attack and attempt to take the dead and injured back to the fort, Lt. Steele sneaks away in a vengeful act to seek Geronimo. He is taken prisoner however and tortured mercilessly by the Indians. In the absence of a father-son relationship between General and Lt. Steele, Captain Starr develops a relationship with the young man and acts as a father figure who attempts a rescue and becomes a prisoner himself. For he is the one who helps Lt. Steele defy his father in an attempt to meet his family. This bond creates another relationship between two white men that leaves Lt. Steele with another sense of loss after Captain Starr sacrifices himself to give the rest of the small band of troops a chance at survival. In addition, this promotes a sense of honor for this character and the army as a whole. Somehow the 16 troops that are left defeat the two-thousand strong groups of various Indian tribes. In addition, due to various languages and lack of relations, these tribes would more than likely never have come together and could not all understand each other. Just because they are Indians does not mean they are all exactly alike in manners of speech and engagement in conflict with the army or white people in general.

Since character development is pivotal in this film, General Steele also evolves based on the loss of his wife and empathy he feels towards his son's fiancé when he visits her in the hospital. He is first portrayed as a hardened military commander who is emotionless and tough as nails. However, as time progresses, he realizes the importance of seeing his son and has actually been trying to protect him by not granting him an assignment. The loss of his wife only furthers his emotional development as he changes his mind about sending troops to rescue his son. He leads a small band out and becomes surrounded by the Indians. This gives him the chance to redeem himself in the eyes of his son and his injury from Geronimo's bullet expresses the importance of what time he has left. In the end, he emerges as a somewhat softer individual who is able to have a relationship with his son.

The white characters in this film experience love, bonds of family and friendship, great loss and sorrow, and are multidimensional, full of depth and range of emotion. The Indians are depicted as war hungry, blood-thirsty, and merciless beings that will stop at nothing to murder the whites. The misrepresentation and social injustices at the Indians' expense continue in this film as they are marginalized and dehumanized. Historical inaccuracies of Geronimo's life also plague this film which is an addition to a growing list of films that attack this man's character and hide the personal experiences of loss and hardship that he faced

Geronimo (Goyathlay), a Chiricahua Apache; full-length, kneeling with rifle.

Photographed by Ben Wittick, 1887.

Courtesy National Archives, photo no. 101 (American Indian Select List)

Chapter 7
Geronimo and the Apache Resistance

Movies have done much to create and perpetuate false myths about Geronimo and the Chiricahua Apache Indians. The documentary *Geronimo and the Apache Resistance* (1988) provides a window in which to view the guarded past of these people and actual descendents are interviewed to correct historical inaccuracies that have tarnished Geronimo's legacy. He was a peaceful man until his family was savagely murdered and only took up arms with his tribe to protect the way of life of his people.

The Apache Indians were never one large tribe but many smaller tribes scattered over a vast geographical area. Geronimo's Chiricahua tribe was one of these small and peaceful groups that never wanted to engage in war but was thrust into conflict to protect their lands and people. In addition, Geronimo was not a war chief but a Medicine Man. The Paramount film from 1940 does a great injustice to his legacy by portraying both he and his people as blood-thirsty and predatory savages that join forces with many other Indian tribes to attack and murder innocent settlers and the army. With many varying languages and cultures, this would most likely never have occurred. Also, the military generally greatly outnumbered the Indians both in men and firepower. In addition, Geronimo never had a personal vendetta against General Crook as the fictional character did against General Steele. He did not desire to mercilessly spill his blood in an act of vengeance. However, both Crook and Steele start out by wishing to truly be at peace with and provide supplies for the Indians. Although with the best of intentions, acts by other military officials, horrible conditions on reservations, and loss of historical lands do not allow for peaceful relations in either the real or fictional case.

However, the movie does correctly express early on the massive media attention given to the attacks at the expense of Geronimo and his people. Both the movie and real-life depictions never accurately presented information regarding the atrocities committed against the Indians. Just as in the movie, accounts of events would emphasize any injuries or deaths at the hands of the Indians but would perhaps gloss over excessive actions by the military. This did much to further the notion that the Apache were savages, but as Mildred Cleghorn expresses in the documentary, "…they had very high moral standards…" The Apache were very much connected to the land and were forced to defend it, for they believed it was alive and gave life. As the commentator states, "The land was beauty, harmony, and power and everything in it was invested with life." Geronimo was a special Holy Man who was also a link to harnessing the power of the land. Somehow, he was able to outsmart the military on so many occasions and was credited with having the power of the coyote to evade the military as long as he did. The land was a great source of power and the cradle of life and culture for the Apache. Therefore, they were greatly disheartened and disconnected as they were forced to leave their land and way of life. In addition, tribes were decimated by hunters who received monetary gains for Indians scalps, for which women and children were not immune.

In March of 1851 as Geronimo was preaching peace, his own mother, wife, and children were murdered by a 400 strong band of Mexican troops. The Apache had no warning and were utterly defenseless; yet, this was not a rare occurrence. Although Geronimo was deeply saddened at his loss and did desire revenge, he was not the vicious and merciless figure that the Paramount film portrays him as. He did not aimlessly murder settlers, he did not strive to kill 1,000 white men, and he did not scalp the dead. He was neither predatory nor blood-thirsty and he was never heavily armed or great in numbers. On the contrary, he and his small band of 39 Apache were mercilessly hunted by an American military troop 5,000 strong. Geronimo and his people were outmanned and outgunned. The military wanted to fight for control over the Southwestern United States; however, the Apache were forced to fight for their very existence. The government wanted power but for the Apaches, the land was power.

While Geronimo fought for the very existence of both he and his people, many other tribes were rounded up and herded like cattle onto reservations. Even some of the Chiricahua Apache not originally in his group were also placed here. Those who fled and were eventually captured or surrendered, endured years of imprisonment with little or no food and water, as well as deplorable conditions that led to massive illness and death. Geronimo's Chiricahua were the last to surrender and endured the fate of being rounded up on trains in horribly cramped conditions where the above-mentioned impending fate awaited them. Some had no idea where they were going, how long they would remain in captivity, or how bad the conditions would be. Families were separated as children were taken from their parents and placed in schools to Christianize or indoctrinate them in the ways of the whites. Separation, illness, death, and longing for the ability to go home and live as their ancestors are all hardships that have resonated through the ages for so many Indian populations.

This documentary corrects the absence of portrayals of valuable relationships, traumatic incidence of loss and hardships, and misrepresentations of the Indian characters in the 1940 Paramount film and others like it. Family members can speak openly of the injustices and hardships that have plagued their people. They are also able to refute the dehumanization by expressing their losses and suffering. It is not merely past generations of Indians that have suffered but also current generations that still feel a sense of loss of identity and coherence. They also still feel a connection to the land that their people once inhabited and that they may never again be able to be a part of.

Geronimo and his small Chiricahua Apache tribe fought for 20 years to protect their lands, culture, and to safeguard their very existence. They also endured atrocities as prisoners of war for another 27 years in horrible conditions where illness and death became daily occurrences. No other individuals or groups of individuals have ever been held for that long a time period. In addition, they had originally been told that they would remain in captivity for only 2 years: They believed that they would eventually be able to return home. However, the final terms of surrender originally agreed to were overturned after the surrender. In addition, the Apache scouts that helped to peacefully bring Geronimo and his small tribe in were also arrested and betrayed by the army. These people were neither predatory savage that acted in an unprovoked fashion, nor were they ever so numerable as compared with the vast army that hunted them. In addition, the so-called warriors of the tribe were in many cases young boys, women, and the elderly, not savage warriors. It was because of the suffering of his people and the massive loss of life that Geronimo was finally urged to surrender under terms that were not honored by the government.

Although this documentary reveals truths and clarifies inconsistencies regarding Geronimo and the Apache Resistance, it can neither correct the massive historical injustices inflicted by the government and the military nor can it restore what has been taken away. However, it can open the door to additional quests for the truth and media attention to publicize what has been so grossly misrepresented through the years. The greatest future injustice, now armed with the ability to discern truth from fiction, will be if we continue to accept: misrepresentations of Indian characters; allow cultural bias; and, make no attempt to preserve the history and culture of these ancient people. Time has inflicted many wounds upon Native American Indians and it is our moral obligation to make every attempt to heal them in the present and in the future

Chiricahua Apache prisoners, including Geronimo (first row, third from right), seated on an embankment outside their railroad car, Arizona.

Photographed by J. McDonald, 1886.

**Courtesy National Archives, photo no. 148
(American Indian Select List)**

Chapter 8
They Died With Their Boots On

They Died With Their Boots On (1941) supports the notion that we have a proud and glorious history as a nation. In reality, the situation is not as simplistic as the filmmakers would have us believe and has nothing to do with the so-called glory they have foisted upon audiences. Through the usage of motivational movie scores and romanticized character portrayals, the stage is set for one to feel a sense of national pride through an otherwise entertaining, yet historically inaccurate film.

The song, *"Garry Owen"* is pivotal in the movie to the establishment of a motivated, unified, and dignified band of 7th Cavalry men under the command of George Armstrong Custer. The adoption of this song in the movie is actually rooted in history, although the title of the song does not represent an actual individual. However, it is actually one word "Garryowen" that is derived from two Gaelic words, "Garrai" and "Oein" that is a literal translation, meaning "Owen's Garden." The historical adaptation for the film is correct in its portrayal that one soldier, full of bottled spirits, bursts into song which then rapidly spreads because it is uplifting and easy to march to. The inaccuracies are that the historical soldier was actually Irish, not British as in the movie and the song was sung around a fire and not a piano in a saloon when it was heard by fellow cavalry men. (AnAmericanSoldier)

    The significant point to remember is that this song is not rooted in American history but was actually the name of a town in County Limerick, Ireland. As Americans, we forget so frequently that this nation has historically been founded with ethnically and racially diverse populations of people. However, as we adapt elements of foreign culture into our own, we have a tendency to forget the true origins. Perhaps this is more of an ironic component of the film because one could argue that the vast majority of current Americans can trace their heritage to other nations. Additionally, it is much more frequently forgotten that this country was already populated by vast and diverse tribes of truly Native Americans that have been incessantly displaced and exploited. As scores of foreign legions of people have flocked to this country, assimilation and integration have occurred for which one can become American; however, those truly native to this country are forced out of ancestral homelands, placed on reservations, and have neither been truly accepted nor have they been represented in a historically accurate fashion. We have forced destruction upon the Indian culture and way of life; whereas, people of other ethnic and racial backgrounds have been added to the melting pot of American society.

    One must also never forget that the expansion of American civilization and industrial progress has occurred through: forcible seizure of Indian lands; death and destruction that have plagued tribal members for which women and children have not been immune; and, through lack of establishment and enforcement of laws protecting Indian populations. The movie does provide a glimpse into the exploitation for profit of the Sioux Indian population in the Black Hills of South Dakota. Custer's nemesis in the film, Ned Sharp, along with his father, are motivated by the almighty dollar and don't want to let a band of Indians be any hindrance to their ability to run profitable trading posts at all military forts. The false gold craze that is started to boost populations of gold seekers and settlers is at the expense of excessive Indian life. Although massive numbers of Indians lose their lives, the losses of the American military soldiers are portrayed, as well as the sorrow experienced by the families, such as Mrs. Custer and Ned Sharp's father. American emotion is dramatized while Indian losses are downplayed. It is believed that Custer himself actually claimed to have found gold, which contradicts the film portrayal. In either case, the craze is started to remove human hindrances to expansion and progress.

Although the historical accuracy and cultural significance of George Armstrong Custer is widely debated, the filmmakers chose a much more romantic and stylized version of his persona. "The entire sequence of events leading up to the Little Bighorn, as well as the battle itself, is fictionalized. In real life Custer very much expected a victory when he attacked the Indian camp." (Wikipedia) One could argue that he is not the gloriously heroic figure as portrayed in this movie rather he could be viewed as a vain, glory-seeking, impetuous, and selfish individual. However, Errol Flynn's character is that of a tall and handsome, charismatic and fearless leader. Custer (Flynn) seems to have fate on his side as he is highly decorated and moves up the ranks to the position of

General very quickly. In truth, the real Custer was never decorated and no papers were mistakenly signed in error, making him a General. Regardless of the controversy surrounding the content of Custer's character and the implications of his actions, he is portrayed as the type of man that other men want to emulate, one that women desire, and the kind of leader that ensures glory even in defeat.

This movie instills a false sense of glory through the usage of uplifting music and romantic dramatizations. However, it falls short on accurate depictions of the consequences of the actions of the military and other expansionists. The fictionalized story leading up to the actual Battle at Little Bighorn immortalizes and glorifies an arguably shady character in American history to the detriment of a widely displaced and exploited population of Indians.

They Died With Their Boots On tells a totally different story that contradicts historical facts. This reflects how Hollywood, until only recently, played fast and loose with American Indian history, culture, and sensibilities. If the producers gave any thought to what Indians in the audiences might have known or felt about how they or their history were portrayed, there is no evidence of it in this film. Movies have been widely sensationalized to increase the entertainment value, at the expense of Native American Indians. This lack of moral and social responsibility has created false historical heroes and has done much damage to the reputations and historical preservation of Indians.

As stated previously, in the movie, "The entire sequence of events leading up to the Little Bighorn, as well as the battle itself, is fictionalized." (Wikipedia) Yet, Custer has become a widely memorialized and celebrated hero to the detriment and dismay of Indian populations and their decedents. Custer has counties named after him in five states, townships in two states, including his home state of Michigan, three additional towns in at least three states, and one locality that is actually named Custerville. He also has a monument in his hometown of Monroe, Michigan, as well as an Indian Reservation named after him that has historically been used for military and law enforcement training. In addition, at Fort Riley, Kansas, the main troop billeting hilltop area is named for him and The U.S. 85th Infantry Division has been given the nickname of "The Custer Division." (Wikipedia)

Perhaps the most upsetting to Indians is a memorial at the site of the battle that made Custer so famous, Little Bighorn, which includes a national park, cemetery, and monument in his honor. Tribes want equal representation in memorial or some means by which the truth can be told and have their dead honored. A descendant and Northern Cheyenne Tribal member, Clifford Long Sioux, visited Little Bighorn and voiced his opinion of the massive structure erected to Custer.

> "But there is no memorial here to Long Sioux's people, only a monument to Custer and his men, a granite monolith atop a flowing, grassy rise. A memorial should have been up many, many years ago to honor the ones we lost....There is little at the battlefield to acknowledge the American Indians who fought....For the Sioux, Cheyenne and Arapahoe, the battle was their last major victory in a long and eventually

unsuccessful fight to save their land from seizure by whites. Even the Crow, allies of Custer, and Arikara, who had scouts who died fighting on Custer's side, believe recognition is lacking." (Bohrer)

Linda Pease who is a Crow descendant whose grandfather was a scout for Custer also said,

"It's a slap in the face to those of us who are descendants...and Native America as a whole, because it appears we may not be regarded equally to other citizens of the United States, still, in 2001....I remember going to the battlefield as a kid and the heroic...Custer was glorified...I remember walking away thinking, that doesn't seem right, but maybe we're not as good as other people....It formed a real negative perception of myself as a Native American....And it does that generation after generation, as well as giving credence to white supremacy." (Bohrer)

Indians don't want to be glorified or memorialized as heroes, they simply want the truth to be told and have the memories of their dead honored. Perhaps this might even help to begin the healing process.

Advocates for memorializing of Indians at the Little Bighorn site, such as former Superintendent Barbara Booher, have been subjected to much public scrutiny. "Her appointment has triggered letters of protest to Washington from Custer fans who claimed she was unfit for the job. Supporters counter that her tenure already has meant more jobs at the battlefield for qualified Indians, and will result in a much more balanced view of the controversial battle." (Bartimus) She also fought for distribution of additional informational resources to clear up historical inaccuracies. Others add that losers of particular battles are generally not memorialized as is the case at this particular site. Unfortunately, even though Custer and his men actually lost, movies have glorified them to the point that even though they lost the battle, they are still considered larger-than life heroes. In addition, Jerry Russell, former president of the 700-member Order of the Indian Wars protested an Indian Memorial because, "They (the Indians) were the enemy." (Looney) There seems to be a great schism between the fans of Custer and those who seek to uncover and promote the truth.

Movie producers, who glorify the white man and vilify the Indian, have done much to perpetuate false myths of historical figures and events. *They Died With Their Boots On* blaringly and irresponsibly immortalizes Custer as a highly heroic figure worthy of so many monuments of worship. Although it is portrayed that Custer falls in battle with his men, are the Indians who fought and died any less worthy of a memorial? Native American Indians could correctly argue that the losses have historically been massive and sustained by so many more Indians than any military personnel or settlers. They might also ask for some sort of disclaimer either prior to or after the movie which allows the refutation of any untrue facts. These people deserve to be memorialized, have their voices heard, and should be given the chance to correct historical misrepresentation to preserve their culture and self-identity before it's too late.

In an egregious final scene, Libbie Custer visits General Sheridan and reads a letter to him left by the fallen Custer, demanding that the government "Make good its promise to Chief Crazy Horse. The Indians must be protected in their right to an existence in their own country." Sheridan, the man who in real life was purported to have said, "The only good Indian is a dead one," replies solemnly to Libbie that, "He has the promise of the Grant administration – from the president himself: - that Custer's demand will be carried out." "Come, my dear," he says in the film's most incongruous and shamelessly fraudulent line, "your soldier won his last fight after all." The irresponsible portrayal of Custer as a champion in pursuit of fairness in treatment of Indians could not be further from the truth.

"The entire sequence of events leading up to the Little Bighorn, as well as the battle itself, is fictionalized. In real life Custer very much expected a victory when he attacked the Indian camp." (Wikipedia) He did not believe, as depicted in the movie, that he and his troops were marching for certain death due to the falsely portrayed aggressiveness and massive number of Indians. He knew that he was outnumbered but perhaps he didn't realize by just how much. Perhaps his impetuous and proud nature prevented him from considering backing down.

Just as in the movie, Custer had been called to testify before Congress, yet the persons involved were actually different. The actions of Secretary of War William W. Belknap and even President Ulysses S. Grant's brother, Orville Grant were being reviewed after the gold rush in the Black Hills that was actually started by Custer. However, in reality, Custer admitted that his testimony was hearsay, unlike in the movie when Custer (Flynn) is forced to make a dying declaration, yet he did give some measure of validation to the accusations. In response, President Grant ordered Custer be arrested which held up an Indian expedition. However, Custer petitioned to be released to march with his troops for which Grant relented.

"As my entire Regiment forms a part of the expedition and I am the senior officer of the regiment on duty in this department, I respectfully but most earnestly request that while not allowed to go in command of the expedition I may be permitted to serve with my regiment in the field. I appeal to you as a soldier to spare me the humiliation of seeing my regiment march to meet the enemy and I not share its dangers." (Wikipedia)

Was it a measure of vanity that prompted this letter to allow his deployment and to save face with his troops? Was it a foolhearted quest for glory that led him into a battle doomed for failure? So many aspects of Custer's persona and actions are debatable; therefore, one can only speculate.

However, "Some sources say that Custer, aware of his great popularity with the American public at the time, thought that he needed only one more victory over the Native Americans to get him nominated by the Democratic Party at the upcoming convention as their candidate for President of the United States (there was no primary system in 1876); this, together with his somewhat vainglorious ego, led him to foolhardy decisions in his last battle." (Wikipedia) This portrays a highly differentiated set of reasons for going into battle knowingly outnumbered between the film and real life events. In reality Custer neither went into battle to ensure the survival of the Indians nor did he do so to protect their treaties with the government as in the film. He went into battle believing that if attacked, regardless of their number, the Indians would retreat under the threat of a strong cavalry. He couldn't be any more incorrect in his assumption. His impetuous actions on the battlefield could be considered murderous and savage and his historically accurate loss does not merit glory.

However, just as in the movie, Libbie Custer did vigorously strive to protect and preserve the heroic persona surrounding her husband. Through many books, she has done much to perpetuate the heroic image. Yet, she did not bargain with government officials to honor a treaty with the Indians. In the movie, she is incorrectly shown offering the dying declaration of her husband as a means of forcing the government to uphold the treaty with the Indians and to give them back land in the Black Hills. In reality she has preserved a false parallel history surrounding her husband and the events of his life. Did she really care about the Indians or did she just want to preserve her own historical persona through her husband? Maybe she realized the embarrassment that would follow if people knew the truth surrounding the events at Little Bighorn. Perhaps she found it much more desirable to be preserved in history as the wife of a glorious military commander rather than that of an impetuous, vain, fool-hearted, egotistical, glory-seeking, and self-centered megalomaniac.

In reality, Custer did lose the Battle at Little Bighorn based on his lack of regard for rules, glory-seeking, and self-centered nature, along with careless and misguided beliefs about the Indians. He did not win as General Sheridan states at the end of the movie to Libbie, "...your soldier won his last fight after all." He was neither a champion of Indian causes, nor was he concerned with their preservation. "The assessment of Custer's actions during the Indian Wars has undergone substantial reconsideration in modern times. For many critics, Custer was the personification and culmination of the U.S. Government's ill-treatment of the Native American tribes." (Wikipedia) Therefore, if memorials to Custer's memory are allowed to remain, equal numbers of historically accurate memorials should be erected to counter the injustices, as is desired at Little Bighorn.

Chapter 9
Little Big Man

To some degree this film, *Little Big Man,* (1970) reverses the usual situation so the whites become stereotypes while the Indians are interesting, individualistic, and unpredictable. In previous films, the Indians have been portrayed as characters of ill repute and plagued with poor qualities that make them lack an heir of morality and humanity. However, in this film the whites are subjected to ill portrayals and take on poor traits of humanity.

At the beginning of the film when Jack and his sister Caroline are left after the attack on their family, she assumes that the Cheyenne Indians will take them to their camp to ravage her. However, this false accusation is baseless as these Indians are good people who wish no harm on Jack and Caroline. The assumption is further expressed when the chief accidentally offers the smoking pipe to her in an act of hospitality thinking that she is a man; therefore, she assumes that the only reason she is not raped is because they initially believed she was a man. Yet, as she sits outside of the camp after everyone goes to bed, she almost seems disappointed that nobody does take her body for pleasure. This is a comically portrayed slight against the widely inaccurate belief that Indians have historically craved white women and would kidnap them to fulfill their sexual desires. Perhaps it is Jack's sister who so greatly desires to be ravaged by the Indian man in this sense.

The next set of characters that can be described as hypocritical are the, *Bible*-beating white settlers, Mr. and Mrs. Pendrake. Although they incessantly preach living by the Christian faith and take young Jack in to indoctrinate him as a proper Christian, the methods each employ can be considered highly questionable. Mr. Pendrake chooses to beat the devil out of young Jack as a means of Christianizing him. However, accepting Christ should be done through the heart, not with the hand. After finding Jack messing around in the hay with a young girl, Mr. Pendrake whips Jack so terribly that he leaves large gashes on his back. Mrs. Pendrake continues to preach the word of the Lord as she treats the wounds and attempts to give merit to her husband's actions by claiming that the path to righteousness can be claimed by his trials. However, from the moment Jack is taken in, Mrs. Pendrake takes on a predatory and pedophilic relationship with him. Although they never engage in intercourse, she takes great pleasure in bathing him and even kisses him much more vigorously than an adoptive mother should. It is only when Jack catches Mrs. Pendrake in a very compromising act of passion in the basement of the soda shop, that it is realized just how much of a hypocritical woman she is, preaching virtuous ways while obtaining evil pleasures on her Wednesday shopping excursions.

Years after leaving the Pendrakes, Jack encounters Mrs. Pendrake again in a house of ill repute and discovers that she has become a prostitute. If any feeling of compassion for this woman were to arise out of the fact that Mr. Pendrake has passed away forcing her to this lifestyle to earn a living, it is extinguished when one recalls the soda shop incident and the comment that if her liaisons were less frequent they might be enjoyable. I don't believe that either Mr. or Mrs. Pendrake could be considered fine, upstanding members of the Christian community. This depiction takes a direct stab at the old practice of Indian Christianization and closes Jack's religion period.

In the next phase of Jack's life as a white man, he accompanies a dishonest swindler, Allardyce T. Merriweather. As Jack states, "After Mrs. Pendrake, his honesty was quite refreshing." Merriweather has a habit of losing limbs as a result of his dishonest ways of salesmanship and penchant for cheating at poker. Perhaps Jack never quite catches on to the business because he has been brought up to be honest by the Indians which is in direct conflict with his expectations to be a dishonest white salesman. Merriweather even expresses that Jack's problem stems from his grandfather, Old Lodge Skins' method of upbringing for which he has not adapted the desire for creature comforts of the white man such as silk shirts. This portrayal of the white swindler directly contradicts previous film depictions of dishonest and plundering Indians as the shady characters.

Perhaps the quintessential portrayal that brings to light former inaccuracies in the movie industry is that of George Armstrong Custer. In *They Died With Their Boots On,* Custer is portrayed as a heroic general who bravely fights the villainous Indians. However, in this film, the arrogant, impetuous, and murderous nature of Custer is more historically accurate than in the Errol Flynn picture.

One could argue that he takes on the role of predatory savage, formerly reserved for the Indians, through the more accurate representation of the Washita and Little Bighorn massacres. Custer is represented in a more true-to life vain form for which he neither deserves nor receives the respect of his troops. In addition, there is no true glory depicted in Custer's actions and he is never referred to as a winner at Little Bighorn. He falls directly in the category of the exploitive and murdering savages that have plagued so many Indian tribes to virtual extinction. Therefore, he epitomizes the antithesis of the peaceful, good-natured humans (Indians) in this film.

In *Little Big Man* the Indians are referred to as humans and the whites are the subjects of harsh representation. This reversal of humanization portrays the Indians as the peaceful and heroic figures and the whites as everything bad and amoral. Jack's inability to adapt to these disreputable white ways, gives further merit to the morality and validity of Indians and to his morally righteous upbringing.

Little Big Man is a tale told by 121 year old Jack Crabb, played by Dustin Hoffman. The conception of Crabb is interesting. Unlike the typical Western hero who serves the interest of progress and expansion in one form or another, Crabb just wants to survive. However, the ideological center of the film is Crabb's grandfather Chief Old Lodge Skins. The chief is played by Dan George of the Salish tribe, and it is through this character that for the first time, an Indian speaks with more than grunts.

Jack is not the typical white hero in films depicting historical events during the dark ages of Manifest Destiny in the United States. In addition, one could argue that regardless of his Anglo biology, he is more of an Indian in spirit than his white appearance expresses. This is the vast difference, one can argue, that being identified as an Indian is not merely based on biology but is based on a spirit that transcends this world into the unknown next. Jack has no desire for wealth, possessions, or recognition in the white man's world. He faces much uncertainty as to where his true place in this world is destined to be. However, he fully realizes that the way of the white man is highly individualistic and not always the path of truth in spirit. The way of his Indian family as a communal society forever fused together to survive against the white man endures great hardships but always perseveres under the guidance of his grandfather, Chief Lodge Skins.

Previous films such as *Ulzana's Raid* and Paramount's 1940 picture *Geronimo,* have portrayed Indians as less than intelligent beings that grunt and moan to communicate. However, in *Little Big Man* the pivotal role of Chief Lodge Skins is that of a highly intelligent spiritual guide who speaks in the most eloquent fashion. The discussions between he and his grandson Jack are the most intimate and touching of all dialogues in the film. Even in the absence of company, Lodge Skins' prophetic dreams maintain the connection to the Little Big Man (Jack Crabb).

The comedic nature of certain discussions of sex between grandfather and grandson instill life into the old Indian character for which he would lack the desirable human trait of humor in previous films. The discussion in which Jack is first rejoined with his tribe and informs his grandfather that he has a white wife, is not only humorous but it also shows the optimistic curiosity that Lodge Skins still has for the whites in the earlier and happier times expressed in the film. As Jack is forced to depart again, he is reassured that in a dream, his grandfather foresees not only his return to the human beings but also the four wives that Jack will acquire. As Lodge Skins states, "It is a great copulation."

When Jack does return, it is a bittersweet reunion as he learns that so many of his Indian family have been killed. In addition, Old Lodge Skins is virtually blinded by an attack for which the scar is highly visible on his neck. Jack asks if his grandfather "hates the white man now" to which Old Lodge Skins replies as he holds a scalp,

> "Do you see this fine thing? Do you admire the humanity of it? Because the human beings, my son, they believe everything is alive. Not only man and animals but also water, earth, stone. And also the things from them like that hair. The man from whom this hair came, he's bald on the other side, because I now own his scalp! That is the way things are. But the white man, they believe everything is dead, stone, earth, animals, and people! Even their own people! If things keep trying to live, white man will rub them out. That is the difference."

Jack stays with his Indian tribe for another year, only being forced to leave after the Washita massacre. During the incident however, Old Lodge Skins refuses to leave his sacred circle in his tee pee. He is not afraid to die and as he says, "It is a good day to die." Old Lodge Skins is a heroic pillar of strength in spirit even though he is becoming an old man who is wounded and blinded by the white man.

In the end, as Jack is returned to his grandfather, Old Lodge Skins once again says, "My heart soars like a hawk." He also tells Jack that he will die soon in yet another eloquent speech,

> "I want to die in my own land where human beings are buried in the sky. There is no other way to deal with the white man. You cannot get rid of him. There is an endless supply of white man but there have always been a limited number of human beings. We won today but we won't win tomorrow. It makes my heart sad; a world without human beings has no center to it."

Jack and his grandfather then head off to the mountain where Old Lodge Skins believes that he will die.

In the mountain scene, grandfather invokes the ancient spirits to allow his death and to stop the human beings for future generations. In yet another brilliant example, he shines as the spiritual center of Jack's world and that of the Indians. Perhaps this is why death refuses him so that he may continue to guide his people in the path of spiritual righteousness in the face of adversity.

Given the violence of the Washita scene, and the change in Jack's character, one expects a change in the remainder of the film. If Washita is to be the structural center of the movie, then it must mark the beginning of the end. Although Jack Crabb lives to tell his story, in the novel he knows that his story ended at Little Bighorn. In the movie, however, we miss that sense of an ending: Jack and Old Lodge Skins wander slowly back down the mountain, as if into the future. Their humorous discussion of sex furthers this sense of ongoing life. What we have at the end, however, is an avoidance of closure, a relapse into comedy when it is least appropriate; the necessary somber note is wholly absent.

Jack is morally wounded after witnessing the widespread massacre of his wives and children, along with so many others of his tribe at Washita. The extremely graphic murderous actions of the cavalrymen and their utter lack of regard for Indian life, does much to darken Jack's heart who once believed the whites to be upstanding and interesting people. However, the unprovoked and indiscriminate slaying of innocent women and children strikes this belief from his mind. He must adapt yet again to survive in the white man's world, regardless of the contempt he holds within.

The massacre at Washita is the pivotal point in the film that changes the tone from that of comedic mockery of the prejudicial, hypocritical, and self-indulgent ways of the white man to one of a dark descent into an incessant quest for survival in his unforgiving world. Jack is no longer sure of himself or where he belongs. Even though he possesses a strong sense of family with the Indians, he is continually forced to coexist in both worlds. Jack even enters Custer's camp and attempts a failed execution on the general who so successfully wipes out his tribe.

Ironically, as Jack's light dims and he becomes disheartened with the atrocities plaguing the Indians, he is forced back into the world of the white man and is reintroduced as an alcoholic. However, it is a famous old gunslinger that gets Jack cleaned up, just long enough to be briefly reacquainted with Mrs. Pendrake and the old swindler Mr. Merriweather. This is the absolute low for Jack as he is shown lying in the mud vomiting his whiskey. The brief encounters perhaps do much to emphasize the turbulent role that the less than reputable white characters play in his darker character development.

However, rather than continue the descent into darkness, Jack reemerges as a lasting character who is able to once again regroup and reenters Custer's camp as a guide. Jack is even instrumental in Custer's decision to attack the Indians at Little Bighorn for which he and his troops are greatly outnumbered and perish. His strength and perseverance in the face of adversity symbolizes the historical plight of the Indians who have had to incessantly regroup and adapt to white man's ways to exist. As Custer is struck down by Younger Bear, he both preserves Jack's life and repays his debt, owed since their childhood. Throughout the film, it appears as though whenever Jack faces adversity, he is in the company of the morally corrupt whites; however, whenever he is saved, he is then depicted back at home with the Indians. One could argue that the path of white progress is the path of darkness and the path of the Indians is honorable and moves in a virtuous path toward the light.

The avoidance of true closure at the end of this film suggests the immortal spirit of the Indians who have persevered spiritually in the face of adversity. For those who are open to acceptance of the true historical representations of the plight of the Indians, there is hope that more will reject these inaccuracies and the injustices that have plagued the once great Indian nations. As Jack and Old Lodge Skins wander down the mountain in the end, the humorous discussion about sex symbolizes continuation through not only physical but also spiritual procreation. The important ties of family and tribal affiliation perpetuate the human population and honor past generations.

Bird's eye view of Sioux camp at Pine Ridge, South Dakota.

Photographed by G. E. Trager, November 28, 1890.

**Courtesy National Archives, photo no. 21
(American Indian Select List)**

CHAPTER 10
DANCES WITH WOLVES

Director Kevin Costner has made a serious attempt to portray the Indian experience from the Lakhota Indian point of view. Indians are actually played by Indians and the Lakhota culture and geography accurately depicted. The Lakhota language is utilized with a remarkable degree of success, and is presented in the gentle, irrepressible humor of 'the People,' a wonderful contrast to the one-dimensional savagery in so many other films. In addition, *Dances With Wolves* (1990) bears a similar theme as *Little Big Man* in allowing the much deserved respect and recognition of the Indians' social structure, morality, and humanity; whereas, the military is portrayed in a more savage and amoral fashion.

The group of Indians portrayed in the film, Lakhota Sioux, originally called themselves An Alliance of Friends which in the Teton dialect translates to Lakhota. In addition, the term Sioux was originally an offensive term given by the French during the time that they were enemies of the Indians, meaning treacherous snakes. The origination was an Ojibwa word for this offensive title nadewisou. (Lakhota) However, the film definitely does not depict a band of savage snakes but a communal society full of cooperation and concern. The time that Dances With Wolves (John Dunbar), played by Kevin Costner, spends with the Indians is peaceful and mutually inquisitive. Conversely, the time that he spends in captivity when he is reunited with American troops is full of prejudice, abuse, and savagery. This is also a shared theme with the film *Little Big Man* in which the central characters both feel a sense of belonging and peace within the world of the Indians and experience a state of conflict in the white man's world.

The basic social unit of the Sioux was the *tiyospe,* an extended family group that traveled together in search of game. (Lakhota) This is portrayed in the film as John Dunbar is awakened by a stampede of buffalo at Fort Sedgewick and quickly rides off to the Indian settlement to notify the eventually appreciative Sioux of their location. Thus a relationship begins and Dunbar becomes more widely accepted by the tribe. However, this also offers one of the first glimpses into a very grim reality for these Indians who so heavily relied on wild game for their very existence. Prior to the successful buffalo hunt, in which only 3 Indians are hurt, the group, including Dunbar happen upon a field strewn with buffalo that have been killed simply for their hides and left to rot in the sun. This is especially disheartening for the Lakhota Sioux who worry about decreasing populations of buffalo and the deferral from regular migratory patterns that they have historically relied on. The Indians rely on buffalo for their very existence, not merely for profit as the whites. This becomes one of the first incidences in the film in which Dunbar really empathizes with his companions and is disheartened by the senselessness of the killings.

In the film, a ritual dance is also portrayed on the evening that Dunbar notifies the Indians of the presence of buffalo. In reality this is a historical practice by the Lakhota Sioux. The Sioux believed in one all-pervasive omnipotent god, Wakan Tanka, the Great Mystery, and religious visions were cultivated. The Medicine Man, or Holy Man, Kicking Bird, played by Graham Greene, would ride off and spend time alone to contemplate his visions to act with enlightened foresight to guide his people. However, the theme of monotheism is not dramatized in the film. Late in the story when Ten Bears urges Dances With Wolves not to leave the village, he says, "You are the only white man I have ever known." This comment suggests that the Lakhota Sioux in the film might not have been monotheistic because of their lack of exposure to whites or to Christianity. The portrayed dance might not have been the symbolic Ghost Dance, which fused old Indian customs with Christianity, yet it is still steeped in tradition.

To appear as realistic and as true to the people as possible, the director, Costner, was also concerned with utilizing actual Indians to play the Indian parts. In addition, the ancestral Lakhota Sioux language is used in the film, along with English subtitles. The accuracy of deliverance of the native language is unparalleled. "Because Lakota contains both masculine and feminine forms of speech, the filmmakers decided to simplify the language by using the feminine form for all Lakota speech in the film. Native speakers of Lakota were reportedly highly amused by hearing warriors and other men in the film speak as if they were women." (Wikipedia) Looking into the eyes of the Native American Indian characters and listening to the beautifully preserved language, has added depth and a humanistic quality previously absent in films that refused to cast actual Indians or that previously disallowed speaking roles.

Understanding the origins in a name, societal structure, religious customs and practices, along with factual Indian portrayals including manners of speech, are all paramount to understanding the overall culture of a population. In addition, being able to view Indians in their actual historical homelands is also instrumental in emphasizing the mystical bond between the natives and the Earth. Filmed on location in South Dakota and Wyoming, the beautiful panoramic views highlight the vast frontier that once allowed Indian populations so much freedom to hunt their precious buffalo and provide for their families. However, so frequently Dances With Wolves withholds the knowledge of the impending population boom of whites along the frontier. When he finally does admit to Kicking Bird of the impending encroachment, he advises that the number of white men will be "like the stars." This is especially disheartening for Kicking Bird after viewing an abandoned camp with mounds of man-made debris and rotting animals. The Indians never kill more than they need to survive and they respect the land both on film and real life.

Throughout the film, Dances With Wolves becomes more firmly planted in the way of life of the Lakhota Sioux. As his observations and beliefs evolve, his words and actions mirror the lives of the Indians, suggesting an additional opportunity for an Indian point of view in the picture. The Indians are a peaceful and moral group that consider themselves true humans. It is when Dances With Wolves goes on the trip with Kicking Bird, after marrying

Stands-With-Fists, that Kicking Bird credits Dances With Wolves with becoming human, as he becomes a highly respected member and protector of the Sioux people. The Indians have loving relationships, as expressed between families, including friends who are also considered extended members. This movie presents itself as a window into the past for which one can really come to know the humanity of these people that still live and thrive today.

Chapter 11
War Party

If the viewer can look past the fact that *War Party (1988)* is perhaps a lower-budget film with less than Oscar-worthy actors, one can focus on the theme of still evident racial tensions between Indians and whites and their quest to co-exist. However, the intent is not merely to emphasize the violence that arises as a result of careless actions in the film. It is a call for understanding that the oppressive environments that Native American Indians live in are not only rooted in history but also present-day problems. An Indian approach to discussing this film would call for understanding, awareness, and an incessant desire for true equality of humanity.

In addition to looking past the highly prevalent and violently dramatized scenes, the viewer must also recognize the portrayal of how different generations of Indians deal with their place in the community among the whites. The central character, Sonny Crowkiller, played by Billy Wirth, despises the fact that his father acts in a subservient and over-accommodating manner to the white mayor. He believes that his father's way is demeaning to their heritage. However, his father tries to represent their heritage in a professional and peaceful manner in his relations with the mayor and town council. This mirrors so many actual stories rooted in history, such as Chief Black Kettle attempting peaceful relations with the whites through treaties and trade, while so many others wanted to stand up and fight the whites rather than live in a state of submission and control. In <u>Bury My Heart At Wounded Knee</u>, Black Kettle lost favor with more passionate members of the Cheyenne who wanted to fight against loss of lands and control rather than believe that the whites would uphold any promises. Ultimately, their concerns were valid as they were nearly completely exterminated in events such as the Sand Creek Massacre and as all populations of Indians continued to lose their sacred lands and ways of life. (Brown) The young Sonny believes that no good can come from being so accommodating to the whites and that relations are not harmonious and above prospective strife.

Unfortunately his feelings are valid even though older members of the community, both Indians and whites, believe that the reenactment of the 100 year anniversary of the fictional Milk River Conflict can bring the town together in celebration. However, Sonny and the younger participants, approach it less enthusiastically. The only elder who actually speaks out about the incident is the old Indian man portrayed as the town drunk, who asks if the women and children who died will be included in the number of participants that will be involved in the reenactment. Although he makes a very valid point, most want to write him off and conveniently forget the true historical nature of the incident, in which so many innocent women and children lost their lives. In reality, he is a Medicine Man, capable of creating a lightning storm later in the film which precedes a revelation of truthful intentions of the whites with relation to punishment for the boys.

Indians would contemplate in wonderment white man's ways of reenacting events in which so many lost their lives in vicious attacks. In the film, the town council argues that reenacting the event will bring tourism their way and thus money for the businesses. However, Indians who had ancestors exterminated at the hands of whites might not see the need to portray such a violent and degrading part of their history. Indians might also argue that the money brought to the town at their expense will not necessarily benefit their people or improve relations with whites. The fact that the dramatized casualties are delegated to be more equally represented between whites and the Indians would also pose a problem and not be historically accurate.

The introduction of the hatchet that once belonged to an ancestor of Sonny's is a sign of the impending violence in the film. It is ripped from history as it is grabbed out of the museum case and thrust into the present, just as unresolved historical issues are reintroduced and perpetuated through senseless acts of violence. Individuals who are unsympathetic to historical oppression and extermination of Native Americans might argue that the excitement of the situation leads to the violence in the film. However, the initial murder of the young Indian by the young white man that arises over a game of pool is wholly premeditated and thought out prior to the reenactment. Although alcohol and marijuana are consumed prior to the battle by both sides, the young white man had already placed the live rounds in his truck prior to arriving at the scene. The excitement of the battle did not cause the first murder of the young Indian man. However, it is the catalyst for additional violence and death. Although the young white man initially murders an Indian, causing Sonny to kill him, it is the whites who band together to savagely murder and scalp the friends of the young Indian. At no time are the whites forced to defend themselves; however, the Indians are thrust into conflict for which they must flee to protect themselves or stand and fight as they are severely outmanned and outgunned.

Sonny and his friend Skitty are all that remain from the war party and find themselves in a position where they have no desirable end to their troubles. Either they surrender and receive 10-20 years for their actions, after the initial lie that they would only get probation, or they can stand their ground and die with honor in the face of adversity. They choose the latter, charge at the National Guard troops, and are gunned down in front of: politicians; the media; family; friends; and, the rest of the townspeople. There never seems to be a desirable end for the Indians. Either they submit willingly and lose their sense of identity and ways of life, along with their lands, or they attempt to fight a losing battle to uphold their honor and lose anyway.

Overall, an Indian review of this film would urge the viewer to look past the over-dramatized violence and poor acting to grasp the underlying themes of struggling to deal with still highly-prevalent racial strife and a kind of damned-if-you-do and damned-if-you-don't approach to relations with the whites. Racial tensions are ever-present by-products of centuries of poor relations between whites and Indians. When incidents occur, such as in this film, old stereotypes and latent prejudices rise to the surface to renew and perpetuate racial struggles. In the end, the Indians are destined to lose but will fight the noble fight to preserve their honor.

Sioux boys as they were dressed on arrival at the Carlisle Indian School, Pennsylvania.

Photographed by J. N. Choate, October 5, 1879.

Courtesy National Archives, photo no. 152 (American Indian Select List)

Chapter 12
The Education of Little Tree

The first theme of *The Education of Little Tree* (1997) is that "You need to know your past."

"As the Cherokee walked farther from his mountains, he began to die. His soul did not die, nor did it weaken. It was the very young and the very old and the sick. At first the soldiers let them stop to bury their dead; but then, more died-by the hundreds-by the thousands. More than a third of them were to die on the Trail. The soldiers said they could only bury their dead every three days; for the soldiers wished to hurry and be finished with the Cherokee. The soldiers said the wagons would carry the dead, but the Cherokee would not put his dead in the wagons. He carried them, walking. The little boy carried his dead baby sister, and slept by her at night on the ground. He lifted her in his arms in the morning, and carried her. The husband carried his dead wife. The son carried his dead mother, his father. The mother carried her dead baby. They carried them in their arms, and walked. They walked further from their ancestral homeland and watched their future die, carried them, and they walked." (Friedenberg)

In the film Willow John, played by Graham Greene, speaks of the "Trail of Tears" which refers to the forced mass exodus of Cherokee Indians to the west in 1838. These human beings, young and old alike were herded like cattle, driven from all of their possessions and precious homeland to land that the whites didn't want. He also spoke of the "paper tree" that held changing words that whites presented to the Indians. This referred to the treaty which his people refused to sign as they attempted to stand their ground with pride, knowing that the white man couldn't be trusted to uphold a treaty or any other promise for that matter. However, some did escape and go back to their homes, such as 8-year-old Little Tree's family.

According to, "Removal Of The Cherokees: The Round-Up 1838," some of those who escaped might have returned home only to find that the white civilians "...came to the Cherokee farms immediately after the soldiers, took the cattle, looted the homes, and burned the houses before the Cherokees were out of sight. They even dug up Indian graves looking for silver pendants." (Holm) Families were separated and forced onto the Trail without being allowed to look for each other. They were not allowed time to adequately prepare for the trip and were utterly taken by surprise. As is the usual case in matters such as these, the U.S. Army possessed the weapons to kill if necessary and employed brute force when their commands were not followed.

These people must have been under great duress; however, their spirit was strong and family honor unbreakable. Their pride and respect for their dead gave them the strength to carry those who perished over great distances, refusing to cart them in wagons once the troops restricted the allowable burial time for those who died on the Trail. It must have been an awe-inspiring sight as well as an absolutely heart-breaking scene. As crowds gathered to watch the Indians pass they wept. What a noble group of human beings, strong in honor and spirit. My heart aches as I picture the scene.

The idea of the "noble savage" has been used by many throughout history. One must fully open up to acceptance of accurate accounts of the treatment of Indians, it can only then be understood that the term savage hardly applies to the Indians. It could however, accurately describe the exploitive, murdering, and callous ways of the whites. A soldier wrote, "I fought in the Civil War and have seen men shot to pieces and slaughtered by the thousands, but the Cherokee removal was the cruelest work I ever knew." (Holm) An absolutely horrid event yes, but unfortunately centuries in American history have been flooded by many "Trails of Tears" and stained by the blood of innumerable Indians.

The second theme of *The Education of Little Tree* (1997) "You need to have a proper education."

> "We walked across a big yard toward some buildings. I could keep up easy. When we got to the door of a building, the lady stopped. You are going to see the Reverend, she said. Be quiet, don't cry and be respectful. You can talk, but *only* when he asks a question. Do you understand?" (Friedenberg)

Although it is important for all children to be given a proper education, the emphasis placed on learning at the Notched Gap

Indian School is not as important as the forced assimilation and adoption of Christian morals and values. In the film, Little Tree conducts himself in a composed and respectful manner, regardless of the overwhelming nature of his surroundings. Like so many generations of Indians before him, he exerts quiet dignity and strength to cope with the burdens placed upon him by the whites. This is the true education that benefits Little Tree, not the rigid study or the horribly imposed punishment of being placed in solitary confinement. Punishment doesn't make him a civilized white it makes him a stronger Indian.

Like so many thousands of other Indian children before him, Little Tree is forced to abandon his true name upon entering the school and is then given the name Joshua. The reverend states, "Americans just don't name their kids after objects." He would neither be allowed to use his given Indian name or speak his native language. In addition to being instructed to abandon his heritage, he is bathed and scrubbed thoroughly and then sprayed like a dog with fleas. His hair is cut and he is forced to don a uniform with clunky old boots that don't allow him to feel the Earth under his feet. Like so many of the other schools for Indians, it was believed that by changing the students' appearance he or she would appear more intelligent and civilized. The first step was forced separation of familial ties; however, the second step was an attempt to separate the child from his Indian soul.

Little Tree is a wonderfully inquisitive and caring little boy who has experienced much that nature has to offer. However, this will lead to a great punishment. While participating in class, the teacher shows pictures of animals and asks what they are doing.

As a couple of students answer incorrectly, Little Tree answers, "They are mating." Although he is correct in his answer, he is viciously beaten with a stick and placed in solitary confinement. With little light and no human contact, except when he is served bread and water, Little Tree agonizes over what he could have possibly done wrong to deserve such a punishment. Each time he is asked he doesn't have an answer because he really doesn't know; however, he is told that he will remain in isolation until he confesses what he has done wrong.

In a touching scene, Little Tree talks to the Dog Star, just as his grandma instructs him to when he leaves for the "school" (prison) whenever he needs to talk to her. Little Tree explains his situation and says it just isn't working out for him and is not a desirable situation. The only time that he is let out is during a play thrown by the townspeople for Thanksgiving, during which he and the other children are forced to wear headdresses made of paper. His friend states that it makes the townspeople feel like they have done something good by throwing the play to overcome their guilt. This is when Little Tree sees his grandpa standing outside the gates to rescue him. Grandpa is able to break the big lock on the gates and comments that it is "just like a prison." It is after this rescue that Little Tree's true education resumes.

The white man's education meant something completely different for the Indian "students." It was an attempt to kill the spirit and commit social genocide among those Indians that still remained after centuries of attempts to wipe them from the face of the United States through rabid expansionism, in the name of progress. A proper education is one that lifts the spirit, not one that suppresses it. It is also one of understanding and acceptance that benefits humanity as a whole. Although it is important for all children to receive a proper education, the term proper does not include forced assimilation and vulgar abuses of power in the name of Christianity.

The third theme of *The Education of Little Tree* (1997) "You need to have a place which is yours."

> "I knew where Granma was taking Granpa. It was to his secret place; high on the mountain trail where he watched the day birth and never got tired of it and never quit saying, She's coming alive! Like each time was the first time he had ever seen it. Maybe it was. Maybe every birthing is different and Granpa could see that it was and knew. It was the place Granpa had taken me first, and so I knew Granpa kinned me. Granma didn't look as we lowered Granpa in the ground. She watched the mountains, far off, and she didn't cry." (Friedenberg)

Little Tree's grandpa tells him that all people need a secret place, "You'll know it when you see it." This is very important as the police attempt to crack down on whiskey distillers who aren't paying the government a share. Little Tree finds his secret place just in time to warn his grandpa, gather up all of the jars, and take them to hide in his newly found spot. He evades capture and is later found by his grandparents with the assistance of his dog, Blue Boy.

Even though this is a clearly-presented theme in the movie, one must look for the deeper meaning in having a secret place. Indians are highly spiritual human beings who believe that the Earth and everything it provides is alive and has a soul. When Little Tree is taken in by his grandparents, one of the first positive changes his grandma makes is removing the old "clobbers" (military style boots). She replaces them with a pair of leather moccasins and instructs Little Tree that it is important to feel the Earth under your feet. Later, when grandpa rescues Little Tree from the Notched Gap School (prison), one of the first things he does when he returns home is remove his boots to feel the bare Earth.

Since Indians believe that they are connected to the Earth from the time of their birth, when they die it is important to be reunited with it. Therefore, when grandpa passes away, there is no better spot than his secret place. The one that gave him so much pleasure as he watched the day give birth so many times but always moved him like it was the first time. Although the loss is painful, grandma's words echo as she instructs, "There are different kinds of dying." Formerly, it meant that one's spirit could perish long before the body. However, in this case, it means that the soul can live on as it is reunited with the Earth. Later when she dies, she believes she will be reunited with grandpa and other ancestors who reside in the Earth in spirit. The burdens of this world are replaced by harmony in the next.

This is such an important lesson in the education of Little Tree, for it emphasizes the power in spirit and overcoming one's troubles with strength and dignity. The promise of spiritual rebirth and renewal offers hope and ensures that he will be reunited with his beloved grandparents in a world of acceptance and harmony. Love and honor transcend this world when the physical body dies. No worldly troubles or impositions can kill one's spirit, for it is a "secret place" that cannot be harmed by the hands of man.

Council of Sioux chiefs and leaders that settled the Indian wars, Pine Ridge, South Dakota.

Photographed by John C. H. Grabill, 1891.

Courtesy National Archives, photo no. 33 (American Indian Select List)

Chapter 13
Thunderheart

Thunderheart (1992) gives viewers plenty to cheer about, but it also presents some of the harsh realities of reservation life that frequently miss the evening news. The Indians that survived centuries of extermination, social genocide, and endured the Trails of Tears were rounded up like cattle and forced onto reservations. Often poverty stricken, reservation life is a struggle with little or no opportunities, high rates of alcohol abuse, and a distrust of the American Government.

Upon first entering the Indian Reservation, FBI Agent Frank Coutelle, played by Sam Shepard, states, "(Sighs) Look at this, we have a third-world slap dab in the middle of America. It's hard to believe huh. It used to be all theirs, clear on up into Canada. This is what they got left." As he and his assigned partner, Ray Levoi, played by Val Kilmer, drive by a group of houses, one immediately notices the dilapidated state of the shelters. The houses hardly seem fit to shelter the inhabitants from the harsh extremes of scorching hot summers and bitterly cold winters in South Dakota. Houses are not all completely furnished with windows. Those that do have them may possess some that are broken, providing no complete shelter from the elements. One might discern that based on the state of the housing, public utilities and comforts such as heat and air conditioning might not be affordable luxuries for individuals who have become problematically and cyclically dependent on the public welfare system.

Surrounding the houses are scant patches of fertile grasses that perhaps have no hope of fully developing as a place for children to run and play. If the Indians on this reservation did possess indoor plumbing, fertilization and hydration would probably be unaffordable luxuries outside. Therefore, children are seen playing in the sandy patches of land around the houses and in the poorly maintained streets. Children are also seen playing, barefoot, amongst massive amounts of garbage strewn across the yards, in the roads, and beyond. If not provided with adequate shots during childhood, this could pose a health threat if injuries arise through cuts as a result of contact with bacterial ridden refuse. Childhood asthma and allergies can also be aggravated as garbage, through various states of decomposition, can irritate these sometimes untreated lung disorders common among children.

Along with the debris, excessive quantities of abandoned cars that surround this community not only litter the landscape, but they may also pose environmental risks as liquid solvents or chemicals still contained within might leak into the soil and inevitably into the drinking water if a public well or pump is used. In addition, with alcoholism rates as high as they are on the reservation, the abandoned vehicles could theoretically provide a desirable hiding place with a clear view of children playing for individuals with abusive intentions to lurk.

There appears to be an observable and somber nature amongst individuals as the two FBI Agents pass through. It is almost an expression of hopelessness brought on by years of plaguing burdens as the older individuals are seen sitting on the porches. For the younger children, one must wonder why they are not in school when it seems as though it is the time of day for them to be in classes. For the young mother seen shaking out a sandy blanket, one must also wonder if she has a husband to provide for her family or if she too is stuck in the bottomless pit of the welfare state.

After investigating the scene where the dead body of Leo Fast Elk is found, they go back through the town, and once again a comment is made about the living conditions but this time by Levoi, "...If they want to do some good, they should clean up the garbage in their front yards first." Once again the extreme poverty is portrayed including: dilapidated wood housing and broken down old trailers; massive amounts of sizable debris; and abandoned old junk cars. However, Levoi blames the state on the Indians, not yet recognizing the role that the United States government has played in their hopeless condition. Ironically however, an American flag hangs very prominently from the front of one of the dilapidated old trailer homes. This is almost reminiscent of the prominent manner in which Chief Black Kettle displayed the American flag given to him by government officials as a sign of protection, which would ultimately lead to the demise of his people. Later, after the capture of Jimmy Looks Twice, the accused militant, a flag is also prominently displayed but is hung upside down in disdain. This blaringly presents the two sides in the

Indian struggle, those dependent upon government assistance, and those who wish to break free and return to the old ways in which the Indians could enjoy freedom and live with pride. Jimmy explains that the upside down flag is a "distress signal," perhaps to emphasize conditions on the reservation and the oppressive environment inhabitants are forced to live in. What little these people do possess is viciously torn apart as the Goons look for Jimmy once again after he escapes. It is almost as though nothing truly belongs to these people.

The next occurrence that gives a glimpse into the deplorable conditions on the reservation occurs after the agents pass by the run-down service station to their motel. As the agents discuss possible "militant" Indians, Coutelle is forced to wash his hands in a filthy sink that spews thick brown gravy-like water. The water seems environmentally harmful for drinking, cooking, and bathing. It appears as though even in those places with indoor plumbing, the environmental nature of the water is suspect.

As the Goons approach the school property, looking for Jimmy, the same disregard for precious possessions of the Indians is once again portrayed as they trash the school in front of many scared children. Compared to our modern-day school districts, the school in this film is very primitive. The school has an outhouse due to a lack of indoor plumbing and therefore, no public waste disposal. In the extreme heat during the summer, the stench must be unbearable. However, compared to running outside in the cold and biting winter winds, one might ponder which is worse. The film presents this school in perhaps a better condition than might actually be in existence but I can only speculate.

Later when Levoi goes to Maggie Eagle Bear's property looking for evidence, it is also full of stick shacks that are barely standing, along with broken down vehicles and piles of debris. The tiny shack that houses Maggie, her grandmother, and six children is hardly enough for one let alone eight people to inhabit. Overcrowding is also an inherent problem for those living on the reservations, in addition to the poor living conditions. Grandma and Maggie also discuss the contaminated water that leads to so many of the children getting sick, as well as to discoveries of dead calves all over the reservation. Therefore, Maggie must take samples of the water for testing.

Grandpa Sam Reaches is a blaring example of deplorable poverty in his little tin trailer with no indoor plumbing or amenities. The ceiling and walls are rusted and water damaged and it appears as though thatch has been added to the roof for extra protection from the elements. The furniture is old and worn, some to the stuffing. He too must go to a well to draw water of questionable quality and carry it to his trailer for drinking, cooking, and bathing. However, he is a respected Medicine Man of the community who is modest and humble and cherishes possessions of meaning such as his 500 year old turtle rattle and his old television set. When Grandpa Sam Reaches reveals his first vision, perhaps it is ironic that over the window in the absence of curtains is an old burlap sack from the U.S. military. Also ironic is the portrayal of conditions that he is forced to live in while there is a teepee just outside of his trailer without a hide for covering to create a true historical Indian shelter, yet inside he also has an American flag.

Later, Maggie Eagle Bear's son is shot and taken to the hospital. Most might not even call it a clinic since it only has one bed and maybe one doctor. Levoi and Maggie are forced to make a bed out of a desk for her son to be treated for his gunshot wound inflicted by the Goons. The hospital is understaffed, poorly equipped, and would hardly meet standards for sanitation. It is also logistically inconvenient and a great distance for most to drive on the reservation. Although it isn't shown in the film, I am skeptical as to whether or not ambulance service is an option. Even if it were, I doubt most would have a phone to have the ability to dial 911. Thus people must drive great distances along dirt roads to receive medical attention, which must be absolutely treacherous in the winter snow.

Finally at Red Deer Table, Levoi and Walter Crow Horse find that they have been test drilling for uranium which explains the contamination in the water. The almighty uranium and mineral deposits seem to supersede human life. This is yet another reminder of the centuries of exploitation at the hands of corrupt whites in the name of progress. This is when the true nature of FBI involvement in the area is revealed and it is made known that they are truly trying to snuff out the ARM (American Indian Movement) members who know too much and who want to improve conditions by freeing themselves from government oppression and exploitation.

The harsh realities presented in this film are so numerous that one can only wonder how we can allow a "third-world country" to exist among so much prosperity. Americans send billions of dollars annually to aid impoverished nations and those affected by disaster. FEMA has the funds and ability to provide temporary housing perhaps much better than the conditions reservation Indians are living in now if people would band together to build decent housing with indoor plumbing, public utilities, and regular trash pickup. Instead of sending so much money abroad, why doesn't the U.S. Government allot a portion of money to make improvements here at home to the truly Native Americans? The injustices and oppressive environments that Indians must still endure never ceases to amaze me as continuous examples remind me that they are still suffering.

    The U.S. government has spent considerable time and effort to change Native Americans. Despite allotment and industrial schools, Native American cultures have not been assimilated into white society. When the film first begins, spiritual images of Indians are seen performing the religious "Ghost Dance" which precedes the savage murder of Leo Fast Elk. This haunting image is seen many times throughout the film to express both the foreshadowing of pivotal events as well as to emphasize the enduring nature of the Indians who still perform the ceremonial dance today. The Indians have never lost their connection to the Earth or abandoned their culture. They have never been fully assimilated into American society but have endured through much hardship, still maintaining strong ties to their past. Perhaps one can argue that the past is truly not separate from these people but surrounds both their physical and spiritual states of being.

    Another significant reference to symbolism in Indian culture is when the two FBI agents, Levoi and Coutelle, investigate the evidence surrounding the body of Leo Fast Elk, Coutelle draws attention to the eagle feather in the circle which is meant to symbolize the ARM. It is presented at various times throughout the film as a significant symbol of an enduring Indian culture. Most all Native American Indians attach special significance to the Eagle and its feathers as images are used on many tribal logos. To be given an Eagle feather is the highest honor that can be awarded within indigenous cultures.

A glimpse of sustained native culture occurs during the discussion between Levoi and Walter Crow Horse, played by Graham Greene, of the "ceremony" that must be performed and the "journey" that Leo Fast Elk must make. The burial ceremony is an example of historically enduring burial practices honoring the dead and preparing them for the journey into their spiritual life where they will be reconnected with their ancestors. This spiritual connection seems virtually unparalleled in modern western burial practices, a true reflection of the pure heart that is sustained through massive trials and tribulations.

This is also the first of many times that the native Oglala Sioux language is utilized by Walter Crow Horse and other characters in the film, which has remained intact regardless of generations of attempts to assimilate Indians fully into American culture, and to force them to abandon their native language. Grandpa Sam Reaches also utilizes this native language so much that Levoi believes it is all he can speak. However, he only speaks English when absolutely necessary, choosing to preserve and uphold his native tongue and treat English as a secondary language of lesser meaning. Had these Indians allowed themselves to be fully assimilated through generations of attempts, the loss of such a beautiful dialect would have been a great tragedy.

The spiritual ceremony of visiting a sweat lodge, accompanied by a holy or spiritual leader is also portrayed in the film. Jimmy, the individual pursued by the FBI asks Coutelle as the agents break up the ceremony, "Do you drag people out of churches when they are praying?" "The sweat lodge represents birth and being born out of the darkness, warmth, heat, wetness, and the small space in the womb. One also crawls out of the lodge. Everything is usually done in a clockwise direction in the lodge. One enters in a clockwise direction, passes rattles clockwise, prayers are given clockwise, and each one leaves clockwise. Most people get their traditional names during the ceremony, and offerings are given of tobacco, food, and other things. There are some variations to the design of the lodge as well as in the general practice; however, the fact that this is a religious ceremony led by an elder, most often a Medicine or Holy Man, remains the same.

The notion of shape shifting is highly prevalent in the film as it is believed by the Indians that Jimmy has the ability to change into different animals to elude capture by the FBI agents, most notably when it appears as though he changes into a deer when the agents believe they have him trapped in an abandoned trailer. In addition, it is also a deer that leads Levoi and Walter Crow Horse into the Red Deer Table to discover the testing trenches that precede uranium mining. This is such an amazingly controversial issue because only in the movies has shape shifting ever been portrayed to the masses, generally in horror films in which a vampire turns into a bat or a human turns into a werewolf. To most, shape shifting is a superstitious belief left to primitive people: There is no such thing in a civilized society. However, metaphorically shape shifting occurs in American Indian culture in song and dance, hunting, healing, and warfare. Only in the white man's world does it take on the dark side, appearing as werewolves and bats. As always, between the Indians and the white man, there is a vast difference in point of view. There is a difference yes; however, the concept and belief across Indian populations is still very much alive, spared from assimilation practices that might deem this concept as sacrilegious in Christianity.

The practice of offering tobacco as a gift to elders is expressed when Walter Crow Horse takes Levoi to see Grandpa Sam Reaches. Since smoking the pipe with an elder is a powerful symbol, the tobacco is a valuable gift to offer. The custom of bartering is also portrayed when Grandpa speaks to Walter and informs him that he wants to trade with Levoi. He wants a trade for Levoi's sunglasses and gives him a rock in return. Perhaps the significance is not necessarily always in that item which is traded but in the act of mutual trade, and in a sense the establishment of a relationship which can further social ties in the community as a whole.

This establishment can be solidified with a tobacco offering or sharing of a pipe in the belief that in doing so, there are no secrets and that one's prayers can be carried to Heaven. I believe it to be highly significant that so many acts of respect and ritual take place in the presence of the elder because their status within the Indian community is highly valuable and central to the community as a whole. Just as Indians believe that there is a center to their existence with reference to the Earth, the Medicine Man or Holy Man seems to serve as the spiritual center for the community.

After the revelation of the vision in which Grandpa speaks of Levoi's childhood strife and embarrassment of his Indian father, there is a festival in which the community seems to come together in celebration, although the reason is not expressed in the film. Customary Indian dress and ceremonial dance, along with music and singing seems to penetrate history and draw it into the present. Although most of the Indians portrayed wear white man's clothing, the historical manners of dress and ritual practice have not been lost to history. Just because an Indian is dressed like a white man, it does not mean he is a white man. Ironically, just as in the scene early on where the large and prominent American flag seems to overshadow a close-up shot of a dilapidated old trailer, and an upside down American flag is displayed at Jimmy's house, so too is a flag displayed at this Indian celebration. It seems to be forever looming over the inhabitants of the reservation as a reminder that they will never be free from the encroachment of white man's ways. However, the flags themselves cannot cover the entire population of people to overshadow their dynamism and resiliency.

In addition to examples of an enduring culture, religion, and language are: discussions of visions; connection to and communications with the Earth; intense bonds of family and community; and extreme faith in spirit in the face of hopeless conditions. People have a tendency to fear that which they do not understand. Since established governments have spent so much time and effort to assimilate Indians into white "civilized" culture, much fruitful knowledge and potential for understanding these ancient native people has been lost. However, it has been lost to most of those outside of the Indian community, not from within. The spirit of these people is pure, just as the film portrays Levoi who in the end gives up his watch to Grandpa. In turn, in a surprising twist, Grandpa somehow sneaks his precious pipe into Levoi's car. His first trade resulted in receiving a rock, for his heart was hardened and spiritually empty. However, in the end his heart was open and on the path to spiritual purity which made him deserving of such a precious and meaningful gift. The Indian way seems nobler than industrialized society and the people more virtuous, resilient, and spiritually pure. No act of governmental oppression or assimilation can break the strong traditions, community bonds, or the values of the Indians. In so many ways, they seem to be the most "human" of all Earthly inhabitants.

Chapter 14
Soldier Blue

Soldier Blue (1970) is an American Revisionist Western that portrays events from the 1864 Sand Creek Massacre in the then Colorado Territory and has received a wide array of mixed reviews. In the New York Times director Ralph Nelson said, "For years it was felt by motion-picture executives that the American public wouldn't accept it, the winning of the west having been part of the visceral myth of our culture. Now I have faith that we've reached a point in our emotional and patriotic development when we can accept a more truthful account of our history. I'm not usually one for violence on the screen, but it has to be, because it is based on fact, and we all feel that it is necessary to emphasize the violence in order to (in)still a national consciousness of the violence that was done to the Indians – a violence that is still being done." (Nelson)

Although the extreme violence depicted in this film is very difficult to watch, it is necessary to SHOCK the viewer into questioning what has been irresponsibly taught in textbooks and negligently portrayed in the media. The viewer should also keep in mind that the portrayals are simply a few reenactments of an exponentially higher number of real-life occurrences. I found myself wanting to cover my face as the tears flowed from my eyes but it would do a great injustice to the memory of generations of exterminated Native American Indians. As I drove home from class shaking and feeling as though I was going to be ill, simply from watching the film, I could only imagine how intensified my feelings would have been if I was actually one of the victims of the Sand Creek Massacre.

Some critics, such as John A. Nesbit, have argued against *Soldier Blue* saying that the film is "Bloody, overrated...fails to stand the test of time." (Rotten Tomatoes) Although I am not an advocate of violence, I don't believe this film is as violent as it could be with respect to honoring the memories of over 500 Indians killed in this massacre by the Colorado State Militia troops, under Colonel John M. Chivington. Violence plagues modern broadcast news and stories deemed especially horrific are repeatedly played, until every last fiber of sensationalism is utilized to draw in viewers. However, why should the horrific incidents of murder, dismemberment, disembowelment, rape, torture, displacement, dehumanization, and countless other acts of extermination of Indians at the hands of whites be hidden from the world?

The answer to the question above is quite simple: The historically accurate, yet emotionally painful depictions must be shown in graphic detail to stress the exploitive nature in which white expansion virtually decimated entire populations of Indians during the establishment of the United States. The West wasn't won, it was taken like a plague of locusts decimates a field of crops. Hopefully Americans can reevaluate the blind patriotism instilled from our earliest youth to include a dual nature of the necessary painful acceptance of accurate historical resolve, along with a cautiously optimistic approach to American patriotism.

Another anonymous critique listed on the website rottentomatoes.com asserted, "...the portrayal of the final massacre is done without the subtlety or insight it deserves." (Rotten Tomatoes) In the earlier stages of the film, there is definitely no indication of the impending graphic violence in the summation, as the love story between Miss Lee and Honus Gent provides comic relief and an heir of sentimentality. However, if this critic believed that the violence of the massacre should have been downplayed or that clues to the impending doom for the Indians should have been presented throughout the film, the overall purpose might have been lost. By shocking the vulnerable and unprepared viewer, just as the Indians were surprised by the troops, he or she becomes open to the possibility that maybe what is believed to be true needs to be challenged. An open-minded state is essential in deciphering truth from fictionalized accounts of what most consider "Indian Wars." However, mercilessly raping, murdering, and dismembering unarmed and ill supplied populations of women and children can hardly be considered war.

Perhaps the director of *Soldier Blue,* Ralph Nelson, was ahead of his time in believing that Americans would be emotionally ready to peel back years of lies and deceit to expose the truths that lie beneath. Unfortunately this film was released during the zenith of the Vietnam War, as well as during the court martial stemming from the My Lai Massacre. The parallels of both the Sand Creek and My Lai Massacres, during which innocent civilians were murdered at the hands of American GI's, was perhaps too much for the public to bear. Unfortunately, the film was banned, once again burying an opportunity to expose dark truths in American History. However, the entire American population does not need to accept it for it to be available for viewing.

How can a citizen of the United States enjoy freedom from censorship but attempt to censor that which is disliked or unpopular because the revealed truths are painful to bear? If you don't want to watch it, you don't have to watch it. If you do, please approach it with an open mind. Don't dishonor the memories of the dead by prohibiting the opportunity for those who seek the truth. This country has prospered from Native American Indians' incessant state of suffering. The time to act is now, for acceptance and accountability is paramount to begin to right the wrongs and end the suffering.

Another critique via <u>Film Chronicle</u> "...the bloodshed and carnage of this beautifully made film are justified by its moral outrage about the white massacre of Indians. The reviewer found *Soldier Blue* a powerful and convincing film." (Rotten Tomatoes) It is refreshing to read a review in which the critic kept an open-mind and understood that the director's purpose was to expose the atrocities of the Sand Creek Massacre. Although it is not known from this brief excerpt whether the reviewer had any prior knowledge or preconceived notion of the actual historical events, the fact that the term "convincing" was used is promising and suggests a lack of bias or prejudice towards Indians.

There are two depictions in the film which I find to be the most disturbing, convincing, and utterly haunting. One is the scene in which the woman is surrounded by a group of soldiers, stripped completely naked, thrown to the ground and raped as laughter fills the air. This woman's spirit is killed and her soul tortured long before the last breath ever leaves her body. The other is the attempt by so many women and children to hide from the horrific violence in a ravine, along with the central heroine and white woman Miss Lee. In a merciless and vulgar display of savagery, soldiers approach and fire round after round after round of bullets into each and every human being to ensure mass extermination of all human souls. As mothers clutch their children and all of the victims huddle together, none possesses a weapon or defenses of any sort. Each innocent person is struck down like metal ducks in a carnival shooting gallery as the soldiers seems to be enjoying it just as much as they would at the county fair. The only survivor from the scene is Miss Lee because she is a white woman, yet her heart still bleeds for the fallen as she sobs and mourns the dead.

I fully agree with the reviewer that these images are morally justified to promote understanding and awareness of the massacre of Indians by the whites. One highly significant occurrence that was not fully developed in the film would have also stressed the broken promises and lackadaisical role of the government in taking any action against outbreaks of violence such as this. Blind faith was placed in the word of government officials that these people would be protected under the American Flag. However, the film could not possibly emphasize enough the large groups of people who sought refuge with the flag for protection and begged for their lives but were mercilessly gunned-down, hacked-up, and savagely mutilated as they symbolically waved the old red white and blue. The director could have depicted over 500 ways to die in this film based on the number of lives lost at the Sand Creek

Massacre. Although too numerous to display all of the atrocities, he chose those which would invoke a psychical response and called for additional discernment between fact and fiction. Hopefully this moral justification will lead to additional revelation and reparations for those still affected by past exploitation and extermination in the quest for progress and expansion.

Conclusion

As I pondered the appropriate closing for this book I happened to catch a story on the evening news about a proposed reconditioning of Mark Twain's books to omit the highly offensive "N" word used against African-Americans. I thoroughly dislike the term but I feel by altering the original state of the books, new readers might forget what a horrible plight Black Americans have endured to emerge from slavery, fight for civil rights, and ensure that equal protections under the law are applied to all citizens regardless of race. If future generations are not faced with the painful truths from our history, I fear the same mistakes might be made.

Just as the "N" word is highly offensive to African-Americans, so too is the term "Indian" considered offensive to some Native Americans who are aware of the origins. "The first Europeans to arrive in North America mistakenly believed they had reached Asia-which they called the 'Indies'-and immediately mislabeled the people they encountered as 'Indians'...Far from being relatively undifferentiated bands of primitive 'savages,' the Native peoples of the New World actually made up one of the most diverse and rich culture regions of the world." (Rasmussen) However, the title has been so widely accepted throughout the centuries that such vast numbers of tribes with varying language, customs, and histories are all lumped into one category "Indians."

Although no offense is meant in employing the widely accepted term, its mistaken inception and oppressive acceptance have made it commonplace in the mainstream. I have chosen to use both "Native American" and "Indian" to connect with all readers who might readily accept both terms to promote awareness and social responsibility in correcting historical inaccuracies. By allowing the media to create and perpetuate inaccurate and damaging stereotypes of Native Americans, future generations might not be able to discern truth from fiction. This could have vast and grave consequences for the numerous tribes that are struggling to preserve their history and culture.

I shall close this book by offering sincere thanks and gratitude for your interest in exploring the concepts that I have chosen to present. My goal in the beginning was to encourage you to question what you have been taught, challenge what you see and hear in the media, and be sensitive to the hardships that centuries of Native Americans have endured. If you maintain an open-mind and an open-heart, then my efforts will have been a success.

Prehistoric pictographs on sand rocks, Adamana, Arizona.

Photographed by D. Griffiths, August 1903.

**Courtesy National Archives, photo no. 143
(American Indian Select List)**

Bibliography

An American Soldier. Garryowen. 17 March 2004. 18 February 2007 <http://anamericansoldier.blogspot.com/2004/03/garryowen.html>.

Bartimus, Tad Associated Press. "New Boss at Little Bighorn Monument Draws Fire From Fans of Custer." 12 August 1990. LA Times. 26 January 2011 <http://articles.latimes.com/1990-08-12/news/mn-944_1_american-indian>.

Bohrer, Becky Associated Press. "Indian Memorial Proves Slow in Coming to Little Bighorn Battlefield." 11 March 2001. LA Times. 18 February 2007 <http://articles.latimes.com/2001/mar/11/local/me-36209>.

Brown, Dee. Bury My Heart at Wounded Knee. New York: Henry Holt And Company, LLC., 1970.

Cruel.com. Employing Redskins as Movie Actors. 19 November 2009. 04 January 2011 <http://www.cruel.com/>.

Dances With Wolves. Dir. Kevin Costner. Perf. Graham Greene and Kevin Costner. 1990.

Dench, Ernest Alfred. The Dangers of Employing Redskins as Movie Actors. 1915.

Geronimo and the Apache Resistance. Dir. Neil Goodwin. Perf. Chiricahua Apaches. 1988.

Geronimo. Dir. Paul H. Sloane. Perf. Chief Thundercloud and Preston Foster. 1940.

Holm, Lamont. Holm Room. 2007. April, March 2007, 2011 <http://www.cliffordholm.info/wb/pages/us-history/1874-trail-of-tears.php#REMOVAL OF THE CHEROKEES: THE ROUND-UP 1838>.

Lakhota. 1995-2011. 17 March 2007 <http://www.lakhota.com/stories/story.history.htm>.

Landis, Barbara. "Carlisle Indian Industrial School History." 1996. 01 April 2007 <http://home.epix.net/~landis/histry.html>.

Little Big Man. Dir. Arthur Penn. Perf. Dustin Hoffman and Faye Dunaway. 1970.

Looney, Ralph. "FINDING TRUE HEROES IN THE 2ND BATTLE OF LITTLE BIGHORN." 11 November 1990. Highbeam.com. 18 February 2007 <http://www.highbeam.com/doc/1G1-156104076.html>.

Rasmussen, R. Kent. American Indian Tribes. Pasadena, CA; Hackensack, NJ: Salem Press, Inc., 1995, 2000.

Rotten Tomatoes. Soldier Blue (1970) . 19 February 2007. 14 March 2007 <http://www.rottentomatoes.com/m/soldier-blue/>.

Soldier Blue. Dir. Ralph Nelson. Perf. Candice Bergen and Peter Strauss. 1970.

Teters, Charlene. Charlene Teters. 26 January 2011 <http://www.charleneteters.com/Welcome.html>.

The Education of Little Tree. Dir. Richard Friedenberg. Perf. Joseph Ashton and James Cromwell. 1997.

The Return of Navajo Boy. Dir. Jeff Spitz and Bennie Klain. Perf. The Cly Family. 2000.

The Searchers. Dir. John Ford. Perf. John Wayne and Jeffrey Hunter. 1956.

They Died With Their Boots On. Dir. Raoul Walsh. Perf. Errol Flynn and Olivia de Havilland. 1941.

Thunderheart. Dir. Michael Apted. Perf. Val Kilmer and Sam Shepard. 1992.

Ulzana's Raid. Dir. Robert Aldrich. Perf. Burt Lancaster and Bruce Davison. 1972.

War Party. Dir. Franc Roddam. Perf. Billy Wirth and Kevin Dillon. 1988.

Welker, Glenn. Chief Sitting Bull. 18 May 2007. 24 January 2011 <http://www.indigenouspeople.net/sittbull.htm>.

BIBLIOGRAPHY

Wikipedia. Battle of the Little Bighorn. 18 February 2007
   <http://en.wikipedia.org/wiki/George_Armstrong_Custer#Battle_of_the_Little_Bighorn>.

—. Controversial Legacy. 18 February 2007
   <http://en.wikipedia.org/wiki/George_Armstrong_Custer#Controversial_legacy>.

—. Dances With Wolves Trivia. 17 March 2007
   <http://en.wikipedia.org/wiki/Dances_with_Wolves#Trivia>.

—. George Armstrong Custer. 18 February 2007
   <http://en.wikipedia.org/wiki/George_Armstrong_Custer#Battle_of_the_Little_Bighorn>.

—. Historical Inaccuracies. 18 February 2007
   <http://en.wikipedia.org/wiki/They_Died_with_Their_Boots_On#Historical_inaccuracies>.

—. Monuments and Memorials. 18 February 2007
   <http://en.wikipedia.org/wiki/George_Armstrong_Custer#Monuments_and_memorials>.

—. They Died with Their Boots On. 18 February 2007
   <http://en.wikipedia.org/wiki/They_Died_with_Their_Boots_On#Historical_inaccuracies>.